Managing
Programming People

Managing Programming People

A Personal View

Philip W. Metzger

Prentice-Hall, Inc.
Englewood Cliffs, NJ 07632

Library of Congress Cataloging-in-Publication Data

Metzger, Philip W., (date)
   Managing programming people.

   Bibliography: p.
   Includes index.
   1. Computer programming management. I. Title.
QA76.6.M474 1987   005.1'068   87-2285
ISBN 0-13-551094-5

Editorial/production supervision
   and interior design: Sophie Papanikolaou
Cover design: Ben Santora
Manufacturing buyer: S. Gordon Osbourne

Cover photo courtesy of the Howard P. Vincent Collection;
reproduction of Daumier's "The Northern Bear"

QA
76.6
.M474
1987

© 1987 by Prentice-Hall, Inc.
A division of Simon & Schuster
Englewood Cliffs, New Jersey 07632

Printed in the United States of America

10 9 8 7 6 5 4 3 2 1

ISBN   0-13-551094-5   025

Prentice-Hall International (UK) Limited, *London*
Prentice-Hall of Australia Pty. Limited, *Sydney*
Prentice-Hall Canada Inc., *Toronto*
Prentice-Hall Hispanoamericana, S.A., *Mexico*
Prentice-Hall of India Private Limited, *New Delhi*
Prentice-Hall of Japan, Inc., *Tokyo*
Prentice-Hall of Southeast Asia Pte. Ltd., *Singapore*
Editora Prentice-Hall do Brasil, Ltda., *Rio de Janeiro*

To

Jeffrey
Cindy
Lori
Scott

with love and pride

Contents

Preface

The manuscript was ready, but my editor screamed: "What's this? There's no preface!"

"I know," I said calmly.

"But," said the editor, "you've got to have a preface!"

"Why?"

The editor sputtered: "Because! All our books have prefaces!"

"But I hate prefaces! Nobody reads them. If you have something to say, better to put it in Chapter 1. Everybody reads Chapter 1."

Exasperated, the editor struggled for control. "Look, do you want to publish this book?"

"I guess so."

"You *guess* so?"

"Sure. Sure, I want to publish it."

"Then gimmee a preface."

"What should it say?"

"How do I know? You're supposed to be the author!"

I thought it over a while. "Look," I said, "the only thing I can think of is to tell people this isn't a technical book . . . "

"Yes, yes, go on . . . "

"That it's about *people* who work on a programming job . . . and about how to manage them."

"Yes, good, go on, go on . . . "

"That's it!"

"You mean that's all? Nothing about how uplifting you think the book will be?"

"You kidding me?"

Introduction

This book is structured in roughly the same way as my text, *Managing a Programming Project* (Prentice-Hall, 2nd ed., 1983). That book follows a programming project's "life cycle" from start to finish, and this book follows the exploits of the characters who populate the life cycle. If you are not familiar with the life-cycle concept, the following should serve as an orientation.

I arbitrarily divide the programming life cycle into six phases: Definition; Design; Programming; System Test; Acceptance; Installation and Operation.

Definition Phase: The problem some customer needs to have solved is defined rigorously and written down. That definition is used as the basis for all ensuing work on the project.

Design Phase: An acceptable solution to the defined problem is conceived and written down as a blueprint for constructing programs.

Programming Phase: A system of programs is written and tested following the blueprint produced during the Design Phase.

System Test Phase: The program system is *retested* by people other than the programmers who produced the programs.

Acceptance Phase: The program system is tested again, this time as a demonstration for the customer, to show that the system precisely fulfills the customer's requirements agreed upon back in the Definition Phase.

Installation and Operation Phase: The program system is installed at the customer's site and put into operation.

Acknowledgments

Three people read the first chapter of this manuscript when that was all there was. Their comments were so encouraging that I decided to go ahead and finish the job. Thanks to Al Pietrasanta, Ivan Gavrilovic, and Bill Perry for their support.

The full manuscript was read by Roy Klaskin, a senior manager at IBM and long-time friend and colleague, and Larry Holland of Holland Associates, friend and associate of more recent years. Both these gentlemen have had more years than they'll admit in all phases of the data-processing business, everything from gofer to manager and all the stops in between. Roy and Larry gently pointed out my errors ("Metzger, that's dumb!") and helped very much to smooth the flow of the book. I appreciate their taking the time from their very busy lives to help out. Naturally, any problems in the book are their fault.

Shirley Porter read the manuscript and give me a bushel of help from the layperson's point-of-view. Unencumbered by any real knowledge of the data-processing field but armed with uncommon common sense, she rescued me from a lot of bad sentence structure and meandering thoughts. If the book does not read well, blame her.

When I finally turned over the manuscript to my editor at Prentice-Hall, he decided to have it reviewed by two authors well known in the computing field. I didn't know their identities until afterward (had they hated my manuscript, I never would have learned their names). Happily, they were both very positive about my book and turned in reports that made me blush. I thank Randall Jensen and Robert Glass mightily for their support and for their suggestions for improvements, which I adopted. They did not know when they read my manuscript that their own books occupy honored spaces on my bookshelf.

My new editor at Prentice-Hall, Bernard Goodwin, was gracious and helpful throughout, and production editor Sophie Papanikolaou and copyeditor Barbara Palumbo did a wonderful job of cleaning up the manuscript and ushering it through all the dark alleys toward final publication. I thank them all. But I want to send a special thank-you to two people no longer with Prentice-Hall, without whose nagging I never would have gotten around to doing this book in the first place: my former editor, Karl Karlstrom, now semiretired, and his former secretary, Rhoda Haas, also semiretired. I have known these two lovely people since they handled my first book in 1973. They have always been helpful, encouraging, and positive, whether shepherding one of my books through production, prodding me to get going on the next one, or arranging for my never-ending royalty advances. Thanks, Karl and Rhoda, and may you both enjoy your new lives.

List
of Illustrations

Daumier, "The Northern Bear," Howard P. Vincent Collection.

Daumier, "Menelaus the Conqueror," Howard P. Vincent Collection.

Magritte, "The Pleasure Principle," Sotheby's, London.

Daumier, "You Are Free to Speak," Howard P. Vincent Collection.

Baldung, "The Fifth Commandment," Kunstmuseum Basel.

Bellows, "Benediction in Georgia," Columbus Museum of Art. Gift of Friends of Art, 1936.

Hausner, "Adam and His Judges," Private collection, Vienna, Courtesy of the artist.

Daumier, "Phédre: 'Mon chere, mes javelots,'" Howard P. Vincent Collection.

The Leaning Tower of Pisa, Courtesy Bob Sparks.

Bruegel, "Parable of the Blind," The National Museum, Naples.

Daumier, "Narcissus," Museum of Fine Arts, Boston.

Goya, "The Third of May," Museo del Prado, Madrid.

Gérome, "Thumbs Down," Phoenix Art Museum, Museum Purchase.

Daumier, "Rue Transnonain," Courtesy of the Art Institute of Chicago.

Daumier, "The Divorcées," Howard P. Vincent Collection.

Delacroix, "Liberty Leading the People," Louvre Museum, Paris.

Daumier, "Three Gossiping Women," Courtesy Wildenstein Gallery, New York.

Villon, "Renée du Trois-quarts," The Baltimore Museum of Art, Museum Purchase.

Daumier, "The Legislative Belly," Courtesy of the Art Institute of Chicago.

Munch, "The Cry," Museum of Fine Arts, Boston. William Francis Warren Fund.

Wood, "American Gothic," Courtesy of the Art Institute of Chicago.

Bellows, "Stag at Sharkey's," The Cleveland Museum of Art, Hinman B. Hurlbut Collection.

David, "Death of Socrates," The Metropolitan Museum of Art, Wolfe Fund, 1931.

Miller, "Jude," Courtesy of the artist.

Managing
Programming People

Daumier, "The Northern Bear," Howard P. Vincent Collection.

The Manager

It was my first new car in quite a while and I was a little disturbed about its performance so far. When it was time for its first checkup, I called the dealer to make an appointment for service and to fix the glitches. The service manager was not nearly as sweet as the salesman had been, and it took some doing just to arrange for an appointment. Finally, I dropped the car off, left a long list of the items needing attention, and left. As I walked past my parked car, my suspicious bone squeaked and I stopped to mark each of the rear tires.

That was a Tuesday morning. Four days later the assistant manager called to tell me my car was ready. Four days for routine items, but, what the heck, they were busy. When I arrived I sought out the service manager and asked for my car. "Sorry, it's not ready," was the reply. "Harry made a mistake calling you so soon. Have a seat, and it'll be ready soon. Hey, Harry . . ."

Two hours later the car was ready. I paid the bill and walked out to my car. I checked the marked tires to be sure they had been rotated. Naturally, they had not been. I went back to the manager and asked why the tires had not been rotated. "They *were*," was the reply. "No, they weren't," said I. "How do you know?" the manager challenged. "I marked them," I said. He glared at me accusingly. His look said, "What a sneaky customer!"

The mechanic was called over. He sheepishly admitted that he had not rotated the tires. He didn't think they needed it. "Did you look over the oil," I asked, "and decide it didn't need it?" "No," he said, "I changed it." I wondered. I wished I had marked the oil. "How about the grease?" I asked. "Of course," he replied. His look said, "Do I look like some kind of crook?"

I finally got the tires rotated and left. By the time I got home I found that a balky seat belt had not been fixed, a muffler rattle was as grating as ever, and the engine was bucking and stalling.

I wrote a three-page letter to the owner of the car agency. (I write a lot more letters now that I have a personal computer.) I sent a copy to the Better Business Bureau, the Consumer Protection Agency, the auto manufacturer's headquarters in Michigan, and a local radio consumer-aid service. I'm the placid type, but these buggers got to me.

Two days later, I got a call from the agency owner. He told me that he had received my letter and wanted to talk it over. "Fine," I said. "Call me Bubba," he said. "Fine," I said. For nearly an hour, long-distance, Bubba tried to persuade me that the things that had happened were just a combination of events that rarely occurred at his agency. He assured me that if I would give him another chance, he would personally see to it that next time I would be satisfied. His pleading got to me, and I said I would consider trying his shop one more time. At the very least, I promised, in return for his taking the time to call me, I would remove from my car's rear window the huge sign saying DON'T BUY FROM BUBBA! There was a low moan at the other end of the line. I had not mentioned the sign in my letter. The truth is, there was no sign. I had not gotten around to it.

Finally, Bubba said he wanted me to know that the mechanic had been reprimanded and had had part of his pay docked. Now I really got steamed. What was wrong with the place was not some poor little mechanic. It was the management. The whole tone of the place was wrong. Among the half-dozen supervisory people I had met there, none gave me the warm feeling that they wanted to make me a happy customer. They were all busy grousing at one another, slamming down phones, passing the buck, being short and exasperated with customers. While there, I witnessed a customer and her salesman having a shouting match. I had even been shuffled from one service manager to a second with a message because the two of them were not on speaking terms!

I told Bubba that he had docked the wrong person, that he should have started with his entire management staff, including himself. I said it was clear that the mechanic who had failed to service my car was only carrying on as was normal for this outfit.

What has all this to do with programming project management? Plenty. In any organization, the manager sets the tone. If the manager does not establish the standards of conduct and performance for the organization, there will be anarchy, discontent, dissatisfied customers, and a bad product. Managers make the difference between humdrum and exciting projects; between discontented and happy employees; between failure and success. I'm always startled when I hear someone claim to like his or her job. The norm seems to be for people to tolerate their jobs, at best, and to hate them, at worst. Invariably, those who like their jobs work in a well-managed atmosphere. The others work for Bubba.

I'd like to describe the attributes I think a good manager should have. I'm well aware there are plenty of managers around, some of them in very high places, who are "successful" in getting a job done, but whose *modus operandi* is to instill fear in their subordinates. They may be world-shakers, but to me they are failures. I have no respect for them. There are too many equally bright and resourceful managers who achieve magnificent results without recourse to fear and bullying.

THE MANAGER AS A MODEL

The manager of a group sets the tone for the entire group. No matter how strong and independent the individuals in the group may be, there is always a tendency to emulate the manager. That places a heavy burden on the manager, but, after all, nobody expects him or her to be divine. The manager's behavior will rub off on those who work for him or her, sometimes in the strangest ways. I had a visit one time from a young programmer and his wife who had come to my home studio to buy one of my paintings. (I was doing a little moonlighting.) I had never met them before. After about a minute's conversation, I knew exactly whom this young man worked for. He used the same clichés, exhibited the same mannerisms, and had even developed the same nervous tic as a certain manager I knew—we'll call him Johnny. I made some remark like, ''You work for Johnny, don't you?'' Surprised, he answered yes and wondered how I knew. After lying my way out, we went on to have a pleasant evening drinking coffee and looking at paintings. The young man could easily have been Johnny's clone.

How a manager goes about setting the tone is sometimes straightforward, occasionally tricky. If you're a decent human being, you'll automatically have a good start. But it takes more than that.

Work A Normal Workday

I mean, if the company's hours are eight till five, be there at eight and go home at five. Wait! Don't throw the book across the room. Just think about it. If you, the manager, make it a habit to stay every evening for an extra couple of hours, don't you think your people are going to get the message? It happens countless times every single day. Eager young employees see the boss slaving away and figure that's how to become boss and make all that money and get that big office where you can while away your evening hours instead of going home and loving the family and mowing the grass. Some pick up the habit out of guilt. It's not fair for me to go home on time while the boss is still working, is it?

Make your occasional late hours the exception, and make sure you

THE MANAGER AS A MODEL

Daumier, "Menelaus the Conqueror," Howard P. Vincent Collection.

let your people know you expect them to get their work done in a normal workday. Adjust workloads so that people can reasonably be expected to finish their work in a normal workday. If you belong to an organization where twenty hours of unpaid overtime each week has become the norm, you'll have a hard time turning things around. Such practices are deeply rooted and rarely questioned You may have to be the one to go to your manager and begin questioning the practice. When you ask to talk to the boss, you might be put off until he or she has time for you that evening.

Maybe you figure I'm talking nonsense. No doubt you can hardly get your work done as it is, while working a lot of extra hours, so how are you going to get anywhere by cutting out the after-hours toil? It took me a very long time to analyze my own work habits and recognize what I was doing. I remember watching others leave when the bell sounded and not only wondering how they could manage it, but being resentful of them as well. The shirkers were fellow managers as well as some of the people who worked for me. Finally, thanks to the accumulated wisdom of the years, I understand some of what I was doing. See if any of this describes you.

First, after years of practice, I found it easy to waste much of my day in bull sessions, long lunches, and pointless meetings. I knew I could get to my real work that evening. I either stayed to catch up or took home a briefcase full of paper. I simply did not use my time productively during the day. Making it up at night or over the weekend became a habit. At the time I deluded myself into thinking I was working hard both day and night, but I wasn't. I was working sloppy, working dumb. And I know I had plenty of company.

Second, I avoided the important decisions by first taking care of the trivia. The important items, usually involving lots of reading, would be taken care of that evening. Much of my day was given over to reading the junk that ended up in my in-basket.

Third, that junk in my in-basket very often was just that: junk. It often could have been ignored and nothing on the project would have been different. When I was new to managing, I had the notion that whatever was sent me had to be read. Why else was it sent? Well, there's at least as much junk in your in-basket as there is in a typical day's mail at home. What you need to do is quickly sort through it, decide what is important enough to demand your reading time, and get rid of the rest. Some of it can be simply thrown away, some can be filed in case you ever do need it, and some can be legitimately sent to someone else. Notice I said *legitimately*. If you send a document to someone else who really shouldn't get it, you'll be putting him or her in the same foundering boat you're trying to escape.

Finally, get rid of the notion that if you don't work those extra hours, you'll miss something and the project will suffer. Believe me, you're just not all that important. It will get done, and done well, if you sharpen your work habits, and by example, the work habits of those around you. What this all amounts to is setting priorities for your time and making very sure that your family life, social life, and personal life are at the top, not the bottom. Can there be the slightest doubt that if your life and your employees' lives away from the job are happier, the job will go better?

Don't Hog the Credit

Someone very smart has said: There is no limit to what can be accomplished if it does not matter who gets the credit. If only politicians subscribed to that thinking! And spouses and parents. And managers.

Be Quick to Praise in Public

When someone does a good job or comes up with a bright idea, jump on it, praise him or her. Of course, you say, doesn't everyone do that? No, a surprising number of managers are very niggardly at handing out compliments. Sometimes that's because the manager *expects* the employee to do a good job, and you don't praise someone for doing what's expected of him or her . . . do you? Well, yes, you do. Plenty of people need to be reassured that they're doing well. They take silence as a negative comment. The only thing you have to lose by passing out praise is a loss of credibility if you overdo it or if you unwittingly hand out praise when it was undeserved. In the latter case, you'll lose credibility with the rest of the troops, because they'll usually know better. They always know if Jerry fouled up before you do.

Another reason some managers are slow to compliment is that they fear the employee will recall the compliment during some discussion of salary. Don't I deserve a raise? You said I did a terrific job. The answer seems obvious. Either Joe is already making a salary in line with the good job he is doing and is expected to do, or he's not and you do owe him a raise. Whichever of those is the honest answer, go with it.

Criticize in Private

Do so gently, firmly, quickly. Make sure you don't let time pass before you tell someone about your displeasure. If he or she is not measuring up to your expectations, say it now, in private, and be sure you understand each other before you part. Such sessions are not fun, but they need not be tragic if dealt with properly. A trap that I have seen many young managers fall into is what I call "saving it up." Because it's tough to call someone in and criticize him or her, these managers make notes for future use when it's time for the employee's yearly appraisal. When the unsuspecting employee asks why am I marked inadequate in Column z, the manager says "Aha! Remember eleven months ago when you were late getting your subroutine in for integration?" The bewildered programmer may have fouled up, but not as badly as the manager who saved up points against him or her.

The worst offense is a *public* criticism followed by a *private* apology. That's like being vilified on page one of the newspaper on Monday for something you did not do, and having the error corrected on Friday in the "beg pardon" section on page eighteen. If an error is made in public, the retraction should be made in public.

Stay Technically Competent

Here I need to address two sets of managers, because the rules are different for each. I'll begin with the first-level managers, the people who actually supervise the programmers, designers, and others who are producing the project's end products.

First-level managers (perhaps called supervisors in your company) need to stay technically sharp and totally involved with the work their people are doing. They need to be so good at programming or designing or writing specifications or devising test cases or whatever it is their people are doing that they are easily able to take over a piece of the job if necessary. They must not follow, nod approvingly, and sign time cards; they must *lead*. There must be no doubt that they completely understand their people's output and are competent to judge its quality. They must be technical leaders. They must teach their less experienced people. And while they're doing all that, they must be learning to manage, to guide, to appraise, to schedule, to make estimates, to budget funds—all those things that at the *next* management levels will consume much more of their time. Doing a good job as a first-level manager is tough. It's one of the most demanding jobs in the company, because you're usually in transition between purely technical work and management, and while you hold this particular job you have to do both. But what an opportunity to show your stuff! You're in a position where you have direct control over a product (a program subsystem, for example), and you have direct control over people. If you can handle that job and deliver a product of excellence and lead a group of happy, productive people enthusiastic about their work, you're a hero (or heroine).

But this road has ruts.

The deepest rut, I think, is the perception that management is the way to grow fastest in the company (more about this later). Many newly anointed first-level managers immediately distance themselves from the nuts-and-bolts technical work and begin empire building. Bad move. You'll have plenty of opportunity to climb that ladder, but don't climb it until there's solid ground under it. Do an outstanding job at the first level. Build your reputation and that of your group by putting out a product that is the envy of all the other managers. At the same time, learn the business of managing.

Some managers distance themselves from the technical work for another reason: They are insecure and feel incapable of both supervising the work and supervising the people. Some who feel this way may never make good managers, but most can overcome their insecurity by being aware of their tendency and taking steps to overcome it. Insist that your people teach you. Watch for instances where you find you don't understand what your worker has just shown you. Maybe it's a logic flow for a new program. Stay with it; don't let it go by and hope the programmer knows what he or she is doing. Have him or her explain it to you until you do understand. Make your subordinates speak to you in your language, not theirs.

I mentioned empire building a while back. Many promising careers are messed up because a new first-level manager hungrily builds his or her group as big as possible as fast as possible. Big means power. Big means success. These people confuse quality with quantity. It's easy to do. A first-level manager, especially in programming, must do everything possible to assure that his or her group stays small, on the order of a half-dozen people. You can't hope to be completely involved in all of their work if you allow the group to grow too large. It's tempting, of course. My, look at me, Mabel. The boss gave me ten more people today. I must be good!

If the boss does try to saddle you with too many people, he'll no doubt be flustered when you're not suitably grateful. Work hard at convincing him or her that it's the wrong move, that it's not the road to excellence. I once had dozens of people reporting to me as a first-level manager. I was proud of my big box on the organization chart, but I had no idea what all those folks were doing for a living. The problem was solved by making me a second-level manager.

One thing more: As a first-level manager, you'll no doubt feel a little schizoid, trying to be both a technician and a manager, but don't become overzealous. Don't try to become your people's guiding light. Keep clearly before you where your supervisory functions begin and end. Stay the hell out of your employees' private lives. A newly appointed first-level manager in my department, as one of his first official acts, sent his staff a memo. Aren't managers supposed to write memos? This one said something like, ''Hello, I'm your new manager and I want you to know I'm here to help you in every way possible to have a successful career; I want you to feel free to call on me for both technical and spiritual guidance. . . . '' Well, we did some fast back-tracking and unspiritualizing. I saw this fellow just

I'M SO BRIGHT I MUST BE A MANAGER!

Magritte, "The Pleasure Principle," Sotheby's, London.

recently standing outside a roadside revivalist tent. Keep out of your peoples' personal lives unless you're invited in. And even then, walk with great care. Try to be helpful, but don't play God. It's tough enough just supervising.

What about technical competence in *upper*-level managers? Here, the story changes. Again, there are a few geniuses who both manage the company and know all the details of the company's products, but that's more likely at McDonalds than at XYZ Computers.

As an upper-level manager, you'll begin to experience some distance between you and the product in terms of detailed understanding. How much distance there is depends partly on your company and its way of operating. One reviewer of this manuscript pointed out that very often even *second-level* managers must be very technically competent, as well as good people-managers. As you "climb the ladder," you'll find some rung at which you'll need to concentrate on the essence of the product, not its

13

ner up you go, the more the balance shifts away from tech-
toward planning, setting goals, measuring progress, ap-
ing, inspiring, hiring, and firing.

time. How do you know what's going on? As a first-level
ix people, you knew exactly where you were. Now you
have to accept more remote evidence of progress. Worse, you have to rely
on people. Excedrin headache number what?

You begin now to develop and use a whole new set of skills.

Start with the understanding that you can't accept too much on faith.
What you need is hard evidence. Lots of books, including mine, talk about
reporting procedures and forms and such, and that's fine but not enough.
You can have the most elaborate reporting and reviewing systems and still
not know the real status of your project. Set up a monitoring structure, of
course, but don't rely on the bar charts and the PERT charts and the verbal
reports and the fancy graphs. Insist on evidence. But what is evidence?

In the case of design specifications or other documents, you have
some obvious evidence. You can look at outlines for the documents, then
later at partial drafts of the documents, still later at completed sections.
You can get a pretty good idea how that particular product is coming along
because you can physically see it, read it. But what about programs? A
logic flow or a listing is not a program. How about a disk or a tape alleged
to contain a program? No help. You're still not seeing anything to warm
your gizzard. How about a logic flow or a listing *and* a disk or a tape *and*
a printed output from the running of the program allegedly on that disk
or tape? Now we're getting warmer.

Let's go back to the design phase, when the program system was
structured. Right there and then is the time when *test* specifications are
also being designed. That's the time for the test specification writers to
designate certain of the tests as ones whose results are to be delivered to
upper management as part of normal reporting procedures. Most of the
time, these tests will be part of the regular testing schedule, but some will
be designed solely for the benefit of managers who need concrete evidence
that things are going the way the bar charts say they are.

Here's an example: Suppose you're a second-level manager. You have
three groups reporting to you, each wonderfully composed of a first-level
manager and five programmers. Each group is responsible for several program subsystems of an overall system called EL WORDO. EL WORDO is
supposed to be the ultimate in word-processing programs for use on a new
line of personal computers called KUMQUAT. A miracle has happened:
You've been given eight months (rather than "have it next week") to produce the first version of EL WORDO, timed to coincide with the availability
of the computer itself.

One of the subsystems is a control program that is to be cycling early with dummy inputs and outputs. There are some 150 separate functions planned for the user of EL WORDO, and each function is handled by a separate program module. Lowest-level modules are to be tested by individual programmers before being combined with allied modules and tested again. Packages averaging fifteen modules each are to be plugged into the control program, one at a time, and tested. Finally, groups of packages, or subsystems, are to be combined with the control program and tested, culminating in a set of tests for the entire integrated system.

Somewhere in there is a level of test, the results of which are appropriate for you to see. Probably it's at the level I've called "package." There are about ten of them. As integration testing proceeds, your plans can call in advance for the results of each of the ten package tests to be formally shown and explained to you, in detail. This is a good distance removed from the lowest level tests, which are the programmers' and the first-level managers' domain, yet early enough in the project that you're not already near delivery time when you spot a problem.

You can include in your planning checkpoints where you actually see tangible results in the form of printed inputs and outputs. The rest of the time you can rely on more conventional written and oral reports. The same process continues up the line. Your manager, for instance, should want to see some subset of the package tests you witness, or perhaps the next higher (subsystem) level of tests.

What else can you do to keep yourself from straying too far from the technical work going on under you? Some things are obvious: frequent briefings from your subordinates; attendance at classes and seminars to keep you up on technological happenings; reading the technical literature. What's not so obvious is that the time for these activities, especially for attending classes and reading, should come mostly out of your workday. It should not be taken constantly from your private life, although sometimes that's unavoidable. If your company is not attuned to the idea of technical education on company time, it's time to pry it out of the Stone Age or find a more enlightened place to toil.

Finally, I think there's something else you can learn that's perhaps as important as anything I've yet discussed regarding fending off technical obsolescence. I touched on it earlier. You need to impress your people with the fact that you want and need to stay abreast of things, and earn their cooperation in helping you to do it. Earn it by showing your willingness to say, I didn't understand that—would you please repeat it? Earn it by being clearly appreciative when they begin to go out of their way to fill you in on something they think you should know. Any decent technician will be tickled to explain to the boss what he or she is doing if the boss really is interested and truly wants to know. A large benefit of all this, aside from keeping you on top of things, is the mutual respect that will inevitably grow between you and your people. The more there is of this kind of communicating, the less impenetrable is the manager/worker barrier.

Invite Criticism and Comment

Once you've invited discussion, make your decisions and get on with the job. I don't believe that any decision is necessarily better than none, as the cliché goes, but I do think it's important to keep moving and not come across as wishy-washy. As a manager, you're paid to make decisions. You cannot possibly know in advance that each decision is going to be a good one, but you've got to choose a path and follow it. You'll sometimes make bad decisions and have to take your lumps, but don't let it paralyze you. No manager of anything, anywhere, is right all of the time. You'll make better decisions more often, however, if you invite discussion. Don't set yourself up as the only one in the department with a brain. Talk less, listen more. You will make a lot more right decisions and gain a lot more respect.

Some managers agonize over every decision, no matter how trivial the subject. A good manager must learn to sort out which are the key decisions, those seriously affecting the fate of the project or the career of an individual or the reputation of the company, and to give them the time and energy and research they deserve. Other matters must be dispatched much more quickly. Managers are expected to be right on most of the important decisions; they usually are forgiven errors on the less important ones.

Push the decision making as low in the management chain as possible, so that a higher-level manager does not waste time wrestling with problems that a lower-level manager might have solved. You can bring this about by (a) letting your subordinates know that you *expect* them to handle some tough ones, and (b) making sure that they know your general direction and philosophy. Suppose, for example, a fuzzy question of ethics comes up. Your subordinates will waste a lot less time wrestling with what to do if they know you are unbending in your views on ethical company behavior.

Take Action Fast to Right a Wrong

You will, believe it or not, do some pretty stupid things now and then. There's only one way out. Don't lie. Don't fake it. Don't try to nail someone else with your mistake. Just admit it, fix it, and get on with life. It may hurt for a little while, but you'll leave behind better feelings and you'll gain respect.

Reward Technical People the Same as Managers

Many technical people who are very good at their jobs become poor managers. They become managers in the first place only because management is perceived to be *the* way up. Most modern companies try to convince their employees that the technical "ladder" is parallel and equal to the managerial ladder. Pay scales are made the same. Equally silly titles are given to each step in both ladders. Equal size offices with equal size windows and wastebaskets are awarded each. Yet the feeling persists that managers are more equal than nonmanagers. Most of the reason for that is that most decision-making is done by managers. Isn't that what managers are for?

Certainly, but not without help. Most managers are not capable of making decisions involving complex technological matters without help—lots of it. Where does the help come from? Partly from subordinate managers, of course, but ultimately from the technical hotshots on the project. The finest technical people on the job should have a dual role: doing technical work and advising management. It's up to management to make sure that the advisory role is understood and honored. It's up to management to promote the best technical people to positions equal in salary and status to corresponding management levels. And it's incumbent on management that the advisory role be a real one, not window-dressing. That means that you, the manager, rely on the technical advisor to help keep you technically current; you seek the advisor's advice on decisions; you include him or her in your management meetings. The advisor may not have a final, decision-making vote, but he or she must have a voice.

Technical advisors in our business have often been used poorly. Part of the reason for this is that managers become quite jealous of their exalted positions and resist having any of their powers eroded by advisors. There is a strong tendency toward cliquishness on the part of many managers, and they often form clubs that are difficult to penetrate—like some silly fraternity where you need a secret handshake to get in. A manager who does not use the tools he has at hand to get his job done in the best possible way is at best misguided, at worst dumb.

Another reason advisors are misused is that we simply have not learned *how* to use them. A couple of people come to mind who illustrate the use and misuse of the advisory role.

Dave was a natural programmer, an excellent technician, but unsociable in the extreme. He had a boiling point of just over 98.6 degrees Fahrenheit. He could, and did, turn out as much excellent code as any four other programmers around him, but don't cross him! There may be a reasonable question whether such a fellow should be tolerated, no matter how good he is—but leave that aside for now. What upper management finally did with Dave, incredibly, was make him a first-level manager! This story is short, because Dave's reign was short. In about a month, after having alienated everyone in sight, and after one of his employees wrote a letter to the company president, Dave was reassigned to an advisory position, which is where he belonged all along, if you grant that he belonged anywhere. The management assignment was a foolish move from the start. Dave did not want it any more than anyone else, but someone thought anyone could be a manager if he or she really tried. I think that's false, and of course, there's serious doubt that Dave ever did try. Making him a manager was not fair to him and not fair to those he managed. It happens that he functioned well in the advisory role.

John was another technical whiz who did not relate well to people. He seemed to do his work at night and then wander the halls by day annoying those who tried to work during normal hours. He loved to bone up on a random subject, then bring it up the next day at the lunch table and dazzle everyone with his erudition. He was generally avoided. And he was made a manager. He lasted until nearly everyone in his group had asked for a transfer. At that point, upper management decided that they had goofed, and changes were made. He was made an advisor, and that worked better, but even an advisor must get along with people and he was eventually consigned to the dungeon and never heard from again.

Instill the Idea of Service

No matter how we earn our living, we all provide a service to someone. We can accept that and be happy doing a good job, or we can resist it as beneath us and have a tough life. More of this later.

THE MANAGER AS A TEACHER

The people who tried managing projects during the fifties and early sixties had some excuse for stumbling. There were few precedents and little accumulated wisdom by which to steer. Things are tougher for you now; you no longer have those excuses. There's plenty of experience to draw on.

A reviewer of the first draft of this chapter commented that "managers are made, not born." A friend who read the remark wondered: Could Salieri have become Mozart, given enough training? Clearly not, but lots of people could become *Salieries*, given enough training, and that's not half bad.

If you're a new manager, you should expect your manager to train you for your job. You should *insist* on it. You'll have the best of it if you can get some formal classroom training *before* you take on your management duties, but that's by no means crucial. There's nothing wrong with learning while on the job, but there's plenty wrong with learning only through unguided groping.

Consider the case of Walter Secondlevel at Super Software, Inc. He is about to promote Jill Whiz to a position as first-level manager of a group of programmers. Jill has been easily the best programmer in her group. She's smart and dependable, and she gets along well with everyone. She enters Walt's office, and he graciously motions her to be seated.

"Coffee?" Walt asks. Jill is a little nervous. She has no idea why she has been called in. Walt buzzes for his secretary.

"Mona," he smiles, "would you get us some coffee and hold my calls?" Mona nods, smiles back, asks Jill how she takes her coffee, and disappears. "Good secretary, that Mona," says Walt. "She fixes a good cup of coffee." Jill smiles weakly and wonders whether Walt ever fixes Mona a cup of coffee.

They chitchat until the coffee is served. Then Walt asks Jill how the job is going, and whether everything is on schedule. Jill shifts a bit in her chair so that she can more clearly see Walt's face around his feet, which are on his desk between them. There's a hole in one shoe and chewing gum on the other. Finally, Walt gets to the point.

"Jill, you've been doing such a terrific job, I've decided to make you a manager."

Jill is thunderstruck, but quickly regains her composure.

"That's wonderful, Mr. Secondlevel," she says. "How much?"

"How much what?"

"How much raise?"

Walt is hurt that she is not so elated over the promotion that money is beside the point. He slides his feet off the desk and scratches his head. He tells her about her new salary, and she smiles and nods. Walt longs for the old days when a woman would have been glad just to get a manager's job even without a raise. They go on to discuss the position and the people Jill will have reporting to her. Finally, she asks:

"How about training, Walt?" It's Walt, now. "I don't know anything about managing, really. When do I go to a management class?"

"Well, we don't have time for that right now. System test is coming up, and nobody can be spared. We'll see about some classes later. Meanwhile, I'll give you all the help you need." Jill left the office with serious misgivings. She had a title, but no credentials.

Down the hall, a similar scene was being played out. Floyd Hotshot was being called into Bill Goodguy's office to receive a similar promotion. When Floyd arrived, Bill was not yet there, so his secretary asked him to have a seat and wait. A moment or two later, Bill Goodguy came into the office carrying a tray with three cups of coffee and the fixings. He set the tray in front of Floyd, shook hands, and invited Floyd to help himself. As Floyd did so, Bill carried the third cup out to his secretary. He returned and sat back comfortably in the stuffed chair next to Floyd.

"Floyd," he began, "you've been doing a whale of a job on EL WORDO. I want you to know I appreciate it." Floyd flushed a bit, smiled, and thanked him for the compliment.

"As you know, the department has grown pretty fast during this past year. We've taken on twenty or so new programmers, and it looks like we'll need even more when this new job comes in." Floyd nodded and sipped his coffee. "Trouble is," continued Bill, "there aren't enough managers to handle the load anymore. We've got too many programmers for each manager, and I'm afraid things will begin to fall through the cracks." He took a long sip from his coffee cup and Floyd waited for him to continue.

"Floyd, I'd very much like you to become a first-level manager and take over the system test group."

Floyd had mixed feelings. He told Bill that he might like that, all right, but he wasn't sure whether he wanted to get away from the technical work.

"I don't want you to, Floyd. I want you to have a small enough group that you can stay right there in the trenches. You'll be a small step removed from the coding pad, but you'll be deeply involved with all of the work your people are doing."

Floyd began to feel excited about the prospects. Like any good technician, he had always known he could manage better than the managers he had seen around him. Here was a chance to do just that.

"What about training, Bill?" he asked. "I think I know how to handle people pretty well, but that's about it. There's a lot more to it than that."

"You bet there is," smiled Bill, as he leaned toward his desk and put down his coffee cup. He sat back comfortably, and for the next hour discussed with Floyd the way he saw Floyd's new job, what his new salary would be, the people he would have in his group, and several other promotions he was making that day. He showed Floyd a new organization chart and explained how he thought all of the new parts would interact.

"One more thing, Floyd," he continued, "I know you love technical work, and I understand your misgivings about managing. If for any reason this job doesn't work out to your satisfaction, I'll see to it that you're switched back to technical work, but you'll stay at the same level and salary. You're ready for promotion in any case, and it was just a question of whether it would be as a manager or as an advisor." Floyd felt a warm glow of satisfaction. He stood and thanked Bill, shaking his hand. He wondered aloud how he would go about getting started as a manager.

"Is there a class I can take?" he asked.

"You bet. In fact, a couple of them, but they don't start for a few weeks. I'll get you scheduled into them. Meanwhile, I'd like you to take this and go somewhere quiet tomorrow and read it through. It's pretty much what I go by." Floyd glanced at the little book Bill had handed him.

"*Managing a Programming* . . . great! I'll start reading it tonight!" They shook hands again warmly, and parted.

Managers are busy people. They're constantly planning, poring over proposals, giving briefings, meeting with customers, attending classes, reading memos, writing memos, appraising subordinates, listening to gripes, and solving problems. Either positively or by default, they're constantly involved in training. Aside from specific training required by many contracts, there are three types of training which ought to concern every manager.

Training Subordinate Managers

Jill Whiz will probably be pretty much on her own, while Floyd Hotshot gets a break. Jill works for a nerd, Floyd works for a man who understands that he's responsible for the sort of start Floyd gets.

As a manager, it's part of your job to train a new manager. It's not simply a generous thing to do; it's in your own best interests. Think selfishly for a moment. Your own success depends on meeting your commitments and delivering quality products. You can't do that alone. And you can't do that if your people are not good at their jobs. You must rely on them absolutely and it is therefore to your advantage to do all that you can to sharpen their competence.

First, discuss with a new manager, as Bill did, how you see your job and how you see his or hers. There's no reason to expect that someone who has worked for your department as, say, a programmer, should automatically understand your motivations. *Tell* the new manager how you feel about the customer, the schedules, the chances for success. Describe your basic ideas about running a programming project. Give the new manager an idea of the framework into which he or she is expected to fit, and at the same time give him or her a chance to object and question where you're headed. Don't expect your new manager to read your mind.

Second, give him or her something to read that describes how you plan to manage—not a description of a particular project, but something a little more generalized. Have you ever thought about writing down in ten or twenty pages your managing philosophy? Try it. It's an experience that makes you *think out*, possibly for the first time, just what your management ideas and values are. If you pattern your operations closely after a model described in a book or manual, give the new manager a copy to read, and allow him or her the time to read it.

Third, enroll your new, green manager in appropriate classes at the first opportunity. Include both administrative classes to help the manager carry out the company's general policies, irrespective of specific projects, and project management classes. Particularly for first-level managers, see to it that they keep their technical skills honed by attending classes and seminars on technical subjects. When anyone in your group attends a class, don't allow the class work to be interrupted. Treat it as if it were as important as anything else that manager might do while on the job.

Finally, try to ease a new manager into the job. Often you can give him or her supervisory tasks before full management responsibilities; sometimes you can team the fledgling with an experienced manager for a while; often you can make him or her your own assistant for a time. Do what you can to make the new job less traumatic.

Training Nonmanagers

I had a disagreement once with a fellow manager over a programmer's reading habits. He came into my office all out of joint because one of his programmers spent a good deal of time reading magazines. I agreed that that belonged outside of working hours, but then I asked *which* magazines were the cause of all this fuss. I expected to hear something ranging from *Playboy* to *The New Yorker*. "Well, technical stuff," he answered. "*ACM*, *Datamation*, things like that." "But what's wrong with that?" I wanted to know. It sounded like a good idea to me. The programmer he was talking about, by the way, was no slouch. My manager-friend said he thought reading ought to be done on the programmer's own time, just as he, the manager, did. I wasn't exactly a flaming liberal in those days, but I thought the manager was surely on the wrong side of this one. I guess I convinced him that the reading made sense—at least, as far as I know, he didn't go out and make a fool of himself by chewing out the programmer.

There are those who are perpetual students. They are always in classes or reading up on the latest what-not. However, only if they never got around to doing their jobs would there be cause to object. In fact, isn't it obvious that you should applaud your people's efforts at improving their skills? Just as in the case of the first-level manager, it's in your best interest for all of your people to be as good at their jobs as possible. Not only should you not discourage continuing training; you should encourage it in every way you can.

I'm not talking only about programmers, designers, and other technically oriented workers. I have in mind secretaries, computer operators, administrative assistants . . . everyone who works for you. Keep an eye out for classes and seminars that might help any of them either to sharpen up what they already know or to learn something of the other person's area. I've always thought, for instance, that it would be a great help to typists, and therefore to programmers, if the typists were to attend a brief class on the basics of programming. Their jobs would be easier and more enjoyable, and probably their output more accurate, if they better understood the jargon programmers write and need typed. Such a minicourse could easily be arranged within your own department, on your own budget. You don't have to look to outside help, because you have the potential teachers already working for you.

And Training Yourself

I said it before: Managers are busy. They tend to go through year after year fighting dragons without time out for their own training. It's always, I can't now . . . too busy . . . do it next year. Pretty soon you begin to pay for not keeping current. For example, you find that you can't communicate well with your programmers. They've gone on to Superlanguage and your mentality is still assembler language bit-fiddling, or at best FORTRAN. You know, you don't have to go to some high-powered course to learn about a new language your programmers are using. Let them teach you! Demeaning? Only if you pompously think you must know more about everything than anybody who works for you. Have Jill Whiz brief you on Superlanguage. She'll be tickled to do it, and she'll see you as a manager who respects her knowledge.

Aside from what you can do with your own resources, there are endless lists of classes offered by your company or by outside consultants. Attend as many as you can that relate directly to your management work, as well as those that are on the fringes or that are not directly related at all. Now we're getting into an area where some of your own time may be involved. The company may not be persuaded to send you to a class on programming of a competitor's computer or to a seminar on writing better memos, but get yourself there anyway.

As a manager, you are constantly concerned about how to pay for things. You have a great deal to do with budgeting money. You must use your influence to include every possible dollar in every budget for various types of *training*. After all, it does not come free. You may find this one of your most difficult chores, because education budgets have a way of starting small and gradually getting axed to death as other, more pressing priorities are felt. Education is often considered a discretionary expense; in a high-technology company, that is extremely short-sighted.

THE MANAGER AS A PROMOTER

There is a very human tendency on the part of most managers to hang on tenaciously to their best people, regardless of whether or not that's good for the employee. An especially enlightened and broad-minded manager will not only allow the transfer of his or her good people to other departments in the company, but will *encourage* such transfers when they are of real advantage to the employee. Most managers moan and snivel and wail and threaten catastrophe if Mary Magnificent, the best programmer in the shop, is offered a job with a promotion in another department, but Manager Bill Goodguy, if he cannot offer Mary as good a position in his own department, will not stand in her way. That's not to say he can ignore his own needs. He'll need to arrange for an orderly transfer so that the work Mary leaves behind in his area does not die when she leaves. But he must not block her promotion, no matter how much it hurts. It's not just that Bill recognizes that nobody is indispensable; it's his duty to watch out for the professional growth of his people. If you assiduously think "employee first, my needs second," everybody wins. Mary certainly wins, for she attains a deserved promotion. Bill Goodguy wins, because he has made a short-term sacrifice for the good of Mary and the good of the company, and has shown himself to be the kind of manager who watches out for the welfare of his people. That kind of reputation goes before him. Bill is the kind of manager people will want to work for.

If you're with me this far, even grudgingly, I'll ask you to take a tiny further step. Don't just go along cheerfully with Mary's promotion. *Propose* your good people for slots you learn about in other departments. Be always on the lookout for opportunities for your people. You say your stomach hurts? Think about it this way: How would *you* like to be treated? How would *you* feel if you were to find out one day that your manager had quashed an opportunity for you to move up? We're not discussing here your timid, run-of-the-mill, self-serving manager who fears any incursion into his fiefdom. We're talking about a manager with the courage to let his people grow, even if they grow right out of his organization.

The kind of behavior I'm discussing is not self-defeating. After all, you don't want to be a martyr. Martyrs are all dead. The behavior I'm advocating will bring you some short-term grief, but long-term rewards. What kind of reputation do you think Bill Goodguy gets? How do you think his ex-workers remember him? And how do you think he feels about himself? You have to choose your managerial life-style: cutthroat selfishness or willing generosity.

THE MANAGER AS A COMMUNICATOR

I mentioned Dave a while back, a washout as a first-level manager. He either could not or would not communicate. He underdid it. Another manager, Gabby, overdid it. He talked a lot and said very little. It was practically impossible to get the gist of what he was saying. Maybe there was no gist. A manager does not have to be the best administrator, the best technician, the best public speaker, but he or she *must* communicate.

There are many styles of communicating. A grizzled old high-school teacher, Smitty, would boom out, "All right, Metzger, dammit! Tell us about the Treaty of Ipswich!" She grinned wickedly through her teeth, and you were ready to recite each day or else you broke your leg and missed class that day. Fear. Intimidation. Another teacher, Mr. Bailey in algebra class, would say, "All right, Philip, please put the answer to this week's special problem on the board." He was so nice that you felt like a traitor if you were not ready and thus betrayed the confidence he had in you. Soft sell.

A new manager can learn a lot about communicating well by reading books on the subject, attending classes, and watching how others do it. In the end, however, how you communicate depends a lot on your personality. Your style is your own. Ignoring style for the moment, we can talk about some of the *kinds* of information that must be gotten across, and how they might be handled.

Job Descriptions

Bees are lucky. They all get very specific jobs. Some clean out the hive, some make war, some bring home the nectar, some get to live it up with the queen. There's one bee whose sole job is to read off job descriptions to the young bees as they first struggle up out of their little hexagonal cells in the honeycomb. He reads off the names and jobs from a computer print-out, and when the last name has been read he goes back to his desk, puts his feet up, and snoozes contentedly until the next batch of young bees is ready.

Managers on a project are not so lucky. Bees emerge from their cells, listen, salute, and off they go to do their jobs. Not so with people. They want to know a lot more. They want to know why Jake goes to visit flowers while they stay home and clean the hive. They want to know who their cell-mates are, what their fringe benefits are, when they're likely to get more nectar. However, they especially want to know what their jobs are.

I mention job descriptions often. That's because I have seen so many people flounder around unsure of their job responsibilities. No doubt some of the people who have worked for me have had the same problem. If I had practiced then what I preach now . . .

A written job description does not have to be a big production. One of the most important reasons for writing it down is that writing forces you to *think*. There is a huge difference between saying that you understand something and actually expressing that understanding on paper. Make a job description fit easily on a single page. Start it with a general statement ('' . . . write, debug, and document program units assigned by your supervisor and present them, complete and ready for integration test, on the dates shown on the master schedule . . . ''), followed by something more specific ('' . . . using coding guidelines in document X, testing procedures shown in test plan Y . . . ''). Or, for an administrative assistant, rather than ''assist management in various administrative tasks . . . '' say ''specifically responsible for scheduling all test time each week for the project, collecting biweekly status reports from each first-level manager and compiling the composite progress report . . . '' I guarantee that you will find that the exercise of writing job descriptions will pay off for you and your employees in terms of a sharpened awareness of expectations and fewer misunderstandings ('' . . . but I thought Jake was collecting the nectar . . . '').

Meetings

Here I want to concentrate on one specific type of meeting, the kind where you convene your whole group, or the whole project if you are the project manager. You have a *dialogue* about the project. You discuss its mission, schedules, problems, achievements, the customer, the project's relationship to the rest of your company, and anything else the people in the group want to discuss. The purpose of this meeting is to get away from managing from the privacy of your cocoon and to exchange perspectives with your people. You let them know what your view of the project is and, if you do your job well, they let you know theirs. On not-so-well-managed jobs, there is a surprising gulf between the two. The workers know what they experience in their own relatively insulated portions of the project and what they hear as scuttlebutt; they do not have the advantage of your perspective. Neither do you see things from their positions. An individual programmer, say, is often privy to information about the project about which you are unaware. He thinks you know all about it, because, after all, you're the manager.

So sit down in a quiet room, all of you together, and talk. You can start things off by giving a little talk, if you wish, about how you see overall progress, but don't make things too structured. Try for freewheeling, uninhibited discussion. Be sure to make clear that that's what is intended in this particular meeting, otherwise it will simply appear to be a bull session and you will look as though you've "lost control."

ENCOURAGING FREE DISCUSSION

Daumier, "You Are Free to Speak," Howard P. Vincent Collection.

Have such a meeting regularly, perhaps once a month. It does not supplant regular briefings and technical walk-throughs. It is in addition to all those other meetings. It's aimed at making a project a family instead of a collection of monks working separately in their little cells.

The Telephone

Everyone knows how intimidating a telephone can be. When you speak over the phone, you're someone different. Hardly anyone comes across the same on the phone as in person. Be aware of this, because it's important to realize that people hearing you without seeing you are not necessarily overwhelmed by what a warm and loving person you are. Record yourself sometime and see if you think that's you on the playback.

There may not be a lot you can do about your basic telephone personality, but there are some things you can do about your telephone etiquette.

Take a look at your office phone. Does it have a bunch of buttons to make you feel important? Does it have one that says HOLD? Think about how you feel when you're put on hold. Isn't it aggravating and just a bit demeaning? Are you and your call not important enough to be heard out without having someone else's call interrupt you? What's the worst that can happen if you eliminate hold? The party trying to reach you will have to call back. Is that so terrible? Or if you must have more than one line, let your secretary tell the second caller that you're busy on another line and you will call back as soon as the other call is completed. You say it's the president calling? President of what? Let him wait his turn!

And what about the people who answer your phones other than you? What kind of impression do they give the caller? It's incredible how many business places you can call and get a rude or unfriendly or dumb reception (or one during which you hear gum-snapping!). When a caller gets anything other than a friendly, businesslike greeting, you've lost stature without even trying.

I know it's been suggested by many people, but really, have you ever tried calling your own office at random times, just to see what reception you get before the answering person knows it's you? Try it. A courteous, cheerful, civil voice at the other end of the phone line is such a tonic, and a blunt, crabby, who-gives-a-damn tone is such a turnoff.

And consider this: You're in your manager's office or you're being interviewed by someone when the phone rings. He or she answers the phone and you sit and wait. Should you not conclude that you are less important than some random caller? Maybe the proper conclusion is that, to get this person's fullest attention, you should telephone rather than have a meeting.

Memos and Letters

Lawyers write in "lawyerese" and thus preserve their jobs. If ordinary people could read legal documents, lots of lawyers would be out of business. Programmers often do the same. In love with their jargon, they shun plain English. Managers who write tons of stilted and wordy memos are just as bad. As Winston Churchill once said of a document presented at a cabinet meeting: "This paper, by its very length, defends itself against the risk of being read."

Most likely, you don't speak in a stilted manner, so why write that way? Make your writing as straightforward as your speech. Instead of a full-page letter saying, "With reference to your invitation to appear before your group to discuss the evolution of the personal computer, let me say that . . . blah, blah . . . " and a couple of paragraphs later, " . . . I therefore am happy to accept your kind offer and . . . blah . . . ," why not say, "Thanks for asking. I accept."

There are courses[1] offered these days on memo-writing and letter-writing. They're worth looking at. If everyone in the business would attend such a course and learn from it, we'd have lots less junk to read.

MAPMAKER AND HISTORIAN

Mapmakers of old were trailblazers. They had to go where there were still bears or sea monsters. When Charles Darwin set out on his travels aboard the *H.M.S. Beagle,* he was simply along for the ride. The real purpose of the trip was to chart seacoasts for future voyagers. While Darwin was enjoying himself getting seasick and riding turtles in the Galápagos Islands, the ship's captain was seeing to it that future ships would find their way.

Do you think your job as a manager is boring? Think of yourself as a sea captain. You've got to get to where you're going in decent time so as not to bankrupt those who sent you, and you have to keep your crew happy so that they don't throw you to the sharks. And before you leave port, you've got to figure out just how you're going to accomplish all of that.

---

[1]There are lots of books, too, on the subject. Try *The Elements of Style,* by Strunk and White. It's delightful.

If only the last guy who traveled this path had left you a map!

Are my ramblings farfetched? When you're given a programming job to manage, you're told more or less where you're going, but not how to get there. One of your first acts of consequence is to construct a roadmap (all right, a *plan!*) to guide you. Your first draft won't be your last. It should get you aimed toward the right continent. Once underway, you take new bearings, find out more about the crew's strengths and weaknesses, and make adjustments to your course. Some months later, you usually arrive where you had intended, although you may have zigzagged your way there.

The *next* time you make that trip, it will certainly be easier. You'll still have to worry about errant winds and different-colored sea dragons, but your basic direction will be sure. Unless, of course, you kept no log of the first trip, or you decided to leave it at home when you set out on the second.

We're getting better at this. We keep better records. We do learn from the last trip, but it's a painfully slow process. In *Managing a Programming Project,* I wail about the need for project historians. If there is anyone in the business doing a good job at history-keeping, I'm not aware of it. What I plead for is conceptually very simple. I won't repeat it all here, just its essence: Managers should make an effort to track their projects in such a way as to be able to relate each new job to those already finished. There is no reason for us to stumble continually over our estimates and develop them out of thin air for each new project. There's all that experience from the last project—why not use it?

If you can't get your company to do some historical tracking, do it yourself. Here's how. Keep accurate records of the major resources you *estimate* that you'll use on your current project. Record each time you significantly *change* any of those estimates, and why. Then record how you actually *expended* resources. At the end, you can compare estimates to actual expenditures. They'll never match, but what's important is that you be able to identify important digressions and the reasons for them. Now you come to the next project and you're ready to estimate its costs. Time to make use of the history you kept from the last project.

If it were all that easy, we would be doing a better job of planning and estimating than we are. The catch is that the next project has to be set up similar to the last one. If you can't view them in parallel, you can't do a lot to compare them and transfer knowledge gained from the old to help you with the new. Again, the solution is conceptually simple. Set up the second project just the way you did the first. Divide it into the same phases, set up the same test hierarchy, call test levels by the same names, call documents by the same names, organize the same kinds of groups—in short, do everything you can to make this project "look" like the one you already finished. Only in that way can you translate needs from the old to the new, and only in that way can you compare the two. The match will never be perfect. No two projects are that alike. However, you can *force* likenesses for the sake of planning and tracking, and can learn plenty from so doing.

The things to keep track of are the major costs, usually staffing and computer time, broken down into categories you can get your hands around. Not simply a big lump called "computer time," for example, but perhaps unit test time, integration test time, system test time, site test time, administrative time. Not just staffing, but programmer-weeks, designer-weeks, and so on. If other items, such as microprocessors or support services, are significant in your business, track their costs as well.

If you keep histories for enough roughly similar projects over a period of months or years, it's possible to extract from them, in time, a coherent set of guidelines for estimating that kind of project.

APPRAISING AND FUNDRAISING

The knock at your office door startles you out of your stupor.

"Yes, come in!"

In walks Harry Hotshot, his face flushed, blood in his eyes.

"Hi, Harry! What's up?" His dander is what's up.

"Boss," he begins through quivering lips, "I'd like to ask you some things about salaries." Omigod, just what you needed. It's been a tough week.

"Sit down, Harry," you say gently, forcing a smile. "Now, what is it you'd like to know?"

"I'd like to know why I do ten times the work that Wally Whiner does and only get paid ten percent more!" Damn! If only these people would keep their mouths shut about their salaries. You have a sudden flashback, and sure enough, there's Wally whining his way into your heart and the company's treasury and wearing you down until he gets a bigger salary increase than he deserves. All the while Wally whines, Harry is at his desk working.

What do you tell Harry? Do you confess that the system is unfair and people are not paid in proportion to their value? Do you admit that there is a big lump of basic salary most people get and that beyond the basic lump there are relatively small adjustments for variations in performance? Will it help to explain to Harry that while his and Wally's salaries right now are not far apart, he needs to think about the future when he'll be promoted to loftier salary ranges while Wally remains closer to what he is now making? Just what is *fair*, anyway?

As a manager, you are constantly involved in the question of salaries for your people. You have the obvious obligation to appraise each person's value as objectively as you can and pay him or her accordingly. But there's more to it than that.

First, there's the difficulty of appraising your people's worth and performance. If you were foreman at an automobile assembly line, the job would be relatively simple. You would be dealing with physical products and could easily determine how well they had been assembled. In the programming business, however, products are not always so tangible. It's clear, then, that you must do something to *make* them tangible. Start by having a written job description for every person who works for you. Write down as explicitly as possible a description of Wally's job. Give him a copy, discuss it, modify it, but make sure that he has in his hands a piece of paper saying what is expected of him. As jobs change, rewrite the job descriptions. If you've never done this, try it. The first thing you'll realize is that it's not so easy, and you'll be tempted to toss it aside. After all, Wally knows what the job is! What you need to realize is that the difficulty in writing the job description only proves its value.

The worst part comes next. You must appraise Wally according to whatever appraisal procedures your company requires. You're immediately faced with the problem that your people are all above average. It's a strange phenomenon. I guess the only answer is that the below average people work for other managers.

It's difficult for some managers to face the fact that, within a given population, some people are "average," some above, some below. Even if you can decide in the quiet of your mind who falls into each category, it's emotionally difficult to tell the average and below-average people that that's what they are. Most people resent being "average" and recoil at being dubbed "below average." The terms are, in their minds, equated to nerd and sub-nerd.[2]

Avoid the use of such terms as *average* and *below average*. It's easier, more positive, and more effective to talk to an employee about his or her strong and weak points. Start with the strong points. Even in your weakest employee, there are some. While teaching watercolor painting classes, I have many sessions during which I critique the students' work. As they

---

[2]On Public Broadcasting's "Prairie Home Companion," Garrison Keillor talks about Lake Wobegon, a place where "all the women are strong, all the men are good-looking, and all the children are above average."

prop their paintings up around the classroom, I do a quick panicky survey to see which ones are going to be toughest to say something positive about. It was desperate work at first, but I soon learned that there are *always* positive things to say ("I see you got the paint on the paper this time, Agnes!"). And as a manager, there are always positive items to underpin your appraisal. Having made a positive start, you can then proceed gently, firmly, to talk about the areas needing improvement ("Maybe you'd like to try sculpture, Agnes").

During an appraisal, after having praised the employee's strong points, it's extremely helpful if you can get him or her to admit and talk about the weak points. If you can make that happen, don't lunge across the desk and yell, "Gotcha!" Instead, show that you appreciate his or her candor, and go ahead with a discussion of the point. ("I think you're right about that, John. Now, let's see what can be done about it . . . "). Make an appraisal session a learning experience for both you and the employee. You should both end the meeting feeling more enlightened about each other's expectations. As I mentioned earlier, however, don't store up goodies with which to whap the employee over the head. Anything serious should be discussed when it first becomes evident, not saved up for an annual appraisal.

What about salary—that's what we're after here. It's important that you appraise your employees relative to each other and relative to your company's standards as honestly as you can, and then peg salaries to those appraisals. There is a tendency on the part of weak managers to push the salaries of both the low achievers and the high achievers toward the middle. That's why Harry Hotshot came boiling into your office. The result of this leveling process is that your hotshot makes perhaps ten percent more money than your more sluggish performer even though the hotshot does ten times the work. If Harry is worth ten Wallys, why isn't he paid ten times as much?

Maybe you cannot change your company's compensation policy overnight, but you should try. Meanwhile, what you *can* do is assure that your best people are paid at the top of their salary ranges and the poorest performers at the bottom. Crusade to make the difference significant, if it is not already. You may think that salary guidelines in your company are static, but that is not likely. The more progressive companies make allowances for the superior performer and provide compensation beyond the normal guidelines, but unless you are a conscientious, probing manager, you might never learn how to buck the guidelines and do the best for your superior workers. Beyond salaries, plenty of companies offer special bonuses or achievement awards. The people who receive such awards generally have an excellent manager pulling for them.

Sas fünfft gebott ift. Su folt niemant tödten.

A COUNSELING SESSION

Baldung, "The Fifth Commandment," Kunstmuseum Basel.

GLUE KEEPER

IBM's Al Pietrasanta reviewed an early draft of this chapter and chided me for giving little attention to the interfaces between people. He wrote, "It is not sufficient for people to do their assigned jobs." I agree. Imagine a well-organized project where thirty people do specific jobs assigned but none speak to one another. Obviously, they couldn't really *do* their assigned jobs without speaking to one another (besides, speaking to each other is part of their job descriptions). Yet if they don't speak to each other at the right times about the right things?

That's where the manager comes in. You need to be alert to what people are doing versus what they are saying so that when you detect a potential conflict you can get them talking to each other. Suppose, for instance, that you have an appraisal session with Pete Programmer and he casually mentions during the conversation that he can't stand Don De-signer. Nothing world-shaking . . . just a little normal human hatred. It seems Don had one time called red-headed Pete a pumpkin.

While you can't always get folks to like one another, you had better see in this case whether you might not bring about a little reconciliation. You may agree that Pete does look rather like a pumpkin, but that pumpkin is writing programs designed by Don. Pumpkin Pete may not do anything to sabotage Don's design, but he's not likely to go to Don to resolve prob-lems either. He'll either work them out his own way, ignore them, or go to Don with a chip on his shoulder and tell him what a dumb thing he did in this design specification.

Take another case: One of your managers responsible for running the computer room writes and circulates a memo telling the various groups needing computer test time that there will be six hours of down time next Tuesday while an equipment change is being made. One of your other managers has a demonstration for the customer scheduled the morning after. The demonstration manager pays no attention—all he wants is his block of time on Wednesday so that he can impress the customer. If his antenna does not vibrate, yours should. A change requiring six hours is probably not minor. The chances that computer operations will be smooth the next day are not 100 percent. Customer demonstrations are important. You'll probably want to alert the two managers to the potential problem and work out different scheduling, either for the equipment change or for the demonstration. It's not enough to assume that everything will go smoothly. The computer manager feels he is doing his duty in letting everyone know about the equipment change; the programming manager has his own concerns and assumes the computer manager will have the computer ready for him at demonstration time; but somebody has to take a little broader view and try to head off a problem by getting the two peo-ple together.

As manager, you need to organize people into neat little groups re-sponsible for very specific products or services; but then you have to run around with a bottle of glue to make sure these groups hang together as a team and don't operate in isolation. It's fine to have your memos and change notices circulating, but that's not nearly enough. You must con-stantly (1) bring your people together in the same room to talk about what they're doing, and (2) listen for daily potential conflicts and bring together the individuals necessary to get them resolved. You know how hairy things get when, say, program interfaces get fouled up; most such problems can be traced back to *people* interfaces that were not managed well.

Norman Augustine illustrates the sort of thing that can happen when nobody is keeping an eye on the players:

On another project, two missile electrical boxes manufactured by different contractors were joined together by a pair of wires. Thanks to a particularly thorough preflight check, it was discovered that the wires had been reversed. It was left to the postflight analysis to reveal that the contractors had indeed corrected the reversed wires as instructed. In fact, both of them had.

CHOOSE YOUR WEAPONS

One of the most important jobs a manager has these days is to choose the tools, procedures, and work schedules that are to be used on the project. In the early days of programming, there was little choice, so this was no big deal. Analysts used narrative and tables and some sort of flowcharts; designers used flowcharts and maybe some tables; programmers, ditto; testers were left pretty much on their own; and everyone routinely was assigned the same working hours. Now there are choices, more of them every year.

It's important that project management choose project tools thoughtfully. Some schemes carry over from analysis to design to programming to testing; it's unwise, therefore, to let each person, or even each group on the project, choose the tools to be used by that person or group. If analysts use HIPO charts and designers use structure charts and programmers use flowcharts, there's going to be a lot of botched communication and lost time, money, and quality on the project.

I'm not pleading for any particular methodologies. You can learn about them from many sources that you will find referenced throughout this book. What I am after is an awareness on the part of the manager that the tools his people use are to be selected consciously, not by default. The tools should be selected for the entire project, not a phase at a time, so that there is consistency from one phase to the next. Sometimes the choices will be heavily influenced by what your people are comfortable with, but that's not going to do forever. There must be a search (never-ending) for the latest methodologies available, and thoughtful decisions concerning their appropriateness for your project.

Not every set of tools will be right for every project. Even something as taken for granted as working hours is deserving of careful attention: Many companies are now operating under flextime, a system allowing employees, within broad limits, to select their own working hours. Although the problems of coordination among people not always at work at the same time may at first seem too onerous, the benefits are substantial: The employee can better accommodate the needs of his own metabolic internal "clock" and become a more content and more efficient worker; increasingly frustrating traffic buildup in the larger metropolitan areas can be significantly eased by spreading traffic to minimize rush-hour jams; the use of limited facilities, such as computers and terminals and even parking and lunchroom areas, can be spread out for more efficient use. The impact on road traffic alone, with the resultant reduction in stress and accidents and lost time, can be substantial. A survey[3] in 1986 showed a significant number of firms offering flextime: Across the United States, 28 percent of employers offered some form of flextime. The breakdown by regions varied from 22 percent in the northeast to 35 percent in the far west.

It's important to understand this: You may study what's available and *still* come up with your own method—perhaps some amalgam of pieces of other approaches. Don't be afraid of that path; nobody claims to have come up with final answers. Don't fear that there's some single solution out there if only you were educated enough to know what it was. The truth is, there are *many* answers out there, perhaps none of them perfect for your job, but some of them may be far better for you than what you're accustomed to using.

MY COMPANY, RIGHT OR WRONG

Whatever else he did, Stephen Decatur surely did us all a disservice in preaching "Our country, right or wrong." There are misguided managers who similarly embrace such fierce loyalty to the *company* that they will do anything to preserve its "good" name. Their transgressions range from rationalizing company weaknesses to covering up company wrongdoings.

There's nothing wrong with feeling and showing loyalty to your company, but don't become blind to its faults. Use your energy to fix the faults rather than defend them.

SURROUND YOURSELF WITH EXCELLENCE

It's difficult for a good manager to believe this, but it's true: Some managers, afraid and unsure, surround themselves with people who are me-

---

[3]*USA Today*, Friday, June 27, 1986. Source: a survey by Administrative Management Society.

SURROUNDED BY EXCELLENCE

Bellows, "Benediction in Georgia," Columbus Museum of Art. Gift of Friends of Art, 1936.

diocre. They do this in order to be perceived as the smartest guy in the group. They are afraid of being outshone by one of their subordinates. What these managers fail to understand is that a manager's job is not necessarily to be the best at everything for which the group is responsible, but rather to build a group of people who individually *are* the best at what they do. The manager's claim to excellence is in finding and effectively using excellent people.

You don't have to pretend anything to your people. You don't have to be as smart at programming as your best programmer or as good a designer as your best designer. You don't feel you should be as fast a typist as your secretary, do you? Think of yourself as an orchestra conductor. Perhaps you were an excellent violinist before becoming conductor, and can still play a mean fiddle, but you can't touch the tuba or the piano or the French horn. As conductor, you surround yourself with the best musicians you can find and afford; you train and plead and cajole and frown and smile and do everything you can to get the musicians to play in harmony; you help negotiate the orchestra's season schedule; you decide what pieces to play and when and how much to rehearse; you assure that what the customers see and hear as they settle back in their seats is a final product that shows none of the agony of its production.

Hausner, "Adam and His Judges," Private collection, Vienna, Courtesy of the artist.

The Analyst

Chapter 2

The story is told that when Gertrude Stein was dying, a hand-wringing friend sat at her bedside and wailed, "Gertrude, oh Gertrude, what is the answer, what is the *answer!*" After suitable reflection, Gertrude rose shakily on one elbow and said, "Damned if I know! What is the *question?!*"

That's what the analyst asks: What is the question? It's his or her job to figure that out. It's somebody else's job to figure out an answer. An appalling amount of effort is wasted in the computer field by people solving the wrong problem.

WHAT THE ANALYST'S JOB ISN'T . . .

Annabelle Analyst works for Fred Freud in the analysis group at Super Software, Inc. She has been recently transferred there from the programming department. Fred and Annabelle meet Monday afternoon in Fred's office. Fred speaks:

"Annabelle, since you're new here, I wanted to see how your conversion from programmer to analyst is going." Annabelle smiles weakly and lets her coding pad slip quietly to the floor. She whacks it out of sight with her foot. Fred continues: "Let's see how we're doing on that problem spec for Floorshine Shoes."

"It's a snap, Fred," replies Annabelle brightly. "Here's a flowchart showing what they need."

Fred squirms a little. "Mmmmm! I see you've already got a solution down. What I'm more interested in right now, though, is just what their problem is. The proposal that got us this job was pretty fuzzy. We need to be sure we know what Floorshine is expecting. . . . "

"I spent all last week at their headquarters and it looks pretty clear to me. They need a KUMQUAT minicomputer at each retail outlet to keep track of the inventory for that store—how many pairs of shoes of each size, style, and color, and so on. Instead of fiddling around shelves in the storeroom, the clerk enters what's needed into the computer terminal and instantly knows whether the store has that shoe in stock, and where to find it."

"And if it's not in stock?"

"What?"

"What if it's not in stock? Is that a lost sale?"

"Gee, I guess so. . . . " Annabelle frowns and bites her lip. Then, brightly: "But Al Sneakers and I—he's my contact at Floorshine—came up with some goodies they're gonna love!" Annabelle spreads her flowcharts on the desk in front of Fred and continues: "We're going to include KUM-ORGANIZE software to allow each store manager to lay out shelves and displays on the screen to make the best use of display space—and the same thing for the storage out back . . . "

"Good," Fred interrupts, "but I thought the main idea here was an inventory control system linking all the stores to the central warehouse so that an item not in stock at the store could be quickly located and sent to the store . . . "

Annabelle glances down at her flowcharts and begins scribbling with a pencil. "Well, if that's what they want, we can easily break in here and . . . let's see, we'll need modems and a system of entry codes into their central computer. . . . "

Fred rubs his forehead and has a fleeting memory of a lake in the Catskills where he has just spent a week's vacation.

"Annabelle," he begins slowly, "you're still programming."

"Sure!" she laughs, "I work for Super Software, don't I?"

"Yes, but . . . tell me, how is it you're talking to this Al Sneakers at Floorshine? Wasn't our contact supposed to be Judy Instep?"

"She was put on another job. They told me to talk to Sneakers."

"I see . . . "

After some nervous beating-about-the-bush, Fred reaches for Annabelle's flowcharts and rolls them up. He leans back with the rolled charts in his right hand and periodically whacks his left palm with the roll as if to punctuate his speech: "Annabelle, it's clear I haven't helped you make the transition from programmer to analyst. You're still in love with the coding pad!" He grins at her, showing a lot of teeth. She stiffens.

"All your career," he goes on, "you've been a problem solver, and a good one, too. But now things are different. You're a problem-definer."

"But the problem seemed so simple. . . . I thought I *had* defined it."

The rest of the afternoon is tough, but by the end of the day Fred and Annabelle have reached an understanding as to what her job as analyst really is. She understands that she must start back at the statement of work in the contract, fuzzy though it is; she understands that she must find the right people at Floorshine to talk to; she accepts the fact that her job is to write a document precisely defining Floorshine's problem.

"And you need to understand that writing the programs is no longer your job," Fred reminds her firmly at the end of their talk. Weary, but enlightened and ready for a fresh start on Tuesday, Annabelle thanks Fred and leaves his office. Fred stands and rubs his eyes and then sees her coding pad under the chair. He picks it up and leafs through it and smiles.

"Nice solution," he mutters. "Too bad it solves the wrong problem."

. . . AND WHAT THE JOB *IS*

First, the analyst must get unanimous agreement from all of the people calling themselves the "customer" about a system some of them think they want built, write down a description of what it is they all think they agree they want, get customer management to sign a document saying yes, this is exactly what we want and yes, that's what we contracted for, or yes, that's what we'd like to contract for, and write the document in such a way that it is accurate, complete, unambiguous, understandable, implementable, and tells what the system is to do without getting into how.

Conceptually, the job is straightforward. In practice, it's a bugger. The analyst is in a deliciously unique position to plant bad seeds early. If the analysis is done poorly, the result will be poor design based on poor analysis and poor programs based on poor design and a poor system containing poor programs. The ripple effect from bad analysis can be devastating.

How do you intelligently choose analysts and avoid sowing bad seeds? Let's look a little more closely at the analyst's job with an eye toward trying to define his or her credentials.

FINDING THE CUSTOMER

Do you think the customer is someone who walks around wearing a customer sign? One of the first difficulties on many projects is figuring out just who the "customer" is.

Annabelle thought she was talking to the customer when she discussed Floorshine's needs with Al Sneakers. However, Al was not the person originally designated as the customer's spokesperson—that was Judy Instep. If you're the project manager or if you're in charge of the analysis team, such a change in customer personnel should instantly alert you. You must immediately talk to your counterpart in the customer's organization and come to an understanding of the meaning of their shift in personnel. Is Sneakers formally replacing Instep on your project? Is Sneakers as qualified as Instep to answer your questions? Was Sneakers in on the project from the start, or must he be brought up to speed? If good old Al is not qualified for the job that he has been thrust into, you're in trouble. You've got to satisfy yourself that the people you are dealing with on all levels in the customer's organization speak for the customer. When there is a question, call on the next higher level in the customer's shop to be sure that the lower-level people you're relying on are the right people. Get things straight now. Otherwise, months from now the boss in the customer's house will ask you, "Who said it was okay to do *that?*"

Every customer has people with differing ideas about problems that they need solved. Al Sneakers may be concerned with what goes on in an individual little store, but his management is looking at a complex of stores and warehouses and how they all can function smoothly to assist one another and boost total Floorshine efficiency. In fact, of course, the customer is generally many people, each responsible for different facets of the business. One person, or group, may be responsible for the formal contract document containing a general statement of work; another may be responsible for signing off on various documents you produce during the course of the project, such as design specifications and user manuals; still another for something fuzzily called "quality control." There may be separate people who arrange for physical work facilities, hardware selection, transportation, security. If you're lucky, there will be someone who pays you periodically. And perhaps separate from all of the people in power, but with a special power all their own, may be the eventual actual users of the system. All of these people may have differing views of what it is you're supposed to be doing for them.

A good contract will spell out who's responsible for what, but a great many contracts don't even address the question. During each phase of the project, you need to be sure that you're dealing with the right people, but during the analysis activity, when you're defining the problem that all the rest of the project will be addressing, it's especially critical to sort out who's who. Al Sneakers may be in over his head and he may scuttle the job for you.

Once the analyst figures out whom to talk to in the customer's shop, he or she needs to keep relationships friendly but not too chummy. This is particularly important if the customer happens to be another department within your own company. Some analysts get in the habit of making informal agreements with a customer, saying, with a wink, Don't worry, we don't need to write that down . . . I'll get the programmers to slip it in. One analyst I knew was an ex-salesman named Willie. He was used to winking. I thought he had some sort of physical problem, but it was just that his face had a permanent crinkle from so much winking. He winked a project right to the edge of the cliff, and only yeoman management intervention saved us from going over the edge.

Finally, treat each member of the customer's organization as though he or she is most important to the success of the project. Don't ignore administrative people who, like the Army's sergeants, often know more about critical day-to-day operations than the brass. Cultivate their friendship and cooperation, but not in a condescending or sneaky way.

UNDERSTANDING THE CUSTOMER'S PROBLEM

Remember: You're there not to dictate to the customer, but to perform a service. You serve your customer best by first understanding his or her problem. You may begin by forming a fuzzy idea of the problem and then correcting your understanding as you learn more and more. You're like the torpedo described by Maxwell Maltz: It has a target and a steering mechanism that constantly causes course corrections to keep it aimed correctly. If the target shifts, sensors in the torpedo determine the amount of shift and cause a course correction to be made on the basis of the sensors' negative feedback. "The torpedo accomplishes its goal by *going forward, making errors,* and continually correcting them." We may hope that the analogy ends just before the target is reached.

There are at least three ways of learning about the customer and his proposed system: reading, interviewing, participating.

Reading

The first thing to read is the contract (or whatever document comes closest to being a contract in your case). Read quickly over the whole thing and then concentrate on that portion of it describing the customer's technical problem. It's usually referred to as the "statement of work." In a perfectly written contract in an orderly world, the statement of work would *be* the problem description and there would be nothing much for an analyst to do. Most often, the statement of work is a starting place providing only a rough outline of the job to be done.

After the statement of work, there will be all kinds of documents to read. Some will be attached to the contract as appendices, some will be working papers of various kinds written by customer personnel or your own proposal team. The analyst will need at least to scan such papers, always keeping in mind that the statement of work is (or should be) definitive, and many of the ideas showing up in other documents may express ideas or opinions that have already been discarded. While your analyst cannot afford the time to absorb every historical tidbit leading up to the award of the current contract, he or she will gain a lot of insight by at least becoming aware of what's gone on before.

Interviewing

Two weeks after Fred Freud's meeting with Annabelle, he calls her into his office again. She sits down and waits for him to speak.

"Where's your coding pad?" Fred asks with a grin. Again with the teeth.

"Coding is for programmers!" she shoots back with a look of mock disdain. They both laugh, and after some chitchat Fred gets to the point.

"I read the draft report you turned in on Friday. It's looking good." Annabelle smiles her thanks. "I'm curious about the blank section on future loads. Having any trouble getting data? Or is it just that you haven't gotten to that section yet?"

"Well," Annabelle frowns and hesitates. "There's a guy in their forecasting department . . . name's Chuck . . . "

"Mmmmm?"

"It's hard to get anything out of him."

"Is he too busy?"

"No . . . "

"Too shy?"

"No . . . "

"Too dumb?"

"Well, no . . . " she says, biting her lower lip. "He answers every question the same way."

"How's that?"

" 'How long is a piece of string?' "

"What?"

" 'How long is a piece of string?' "

Fred rolls his eyes heavenward and leans far back in his chair. "Real deep thinker, huh? I've known guys like that—afraid to go on record about anything. Instead of giving you their best estimates, they'll wear you down until you get so frustrated you make your own."

After a pause, Fred leans forward.

"What we'll do," he grins, "is retitle that section. Call it section 4.1.1, 'How long is a piece of string?,' and leave it blank. We'll soon get some action. . . . Seriously, we need to get that information through Chuck rather than going around him, if that's possible. Don't want to make anybody hostile."

"Maybe he already is hostile. . . . "

"Doubt it. Just another guy trying to cover his butt. Afraid to make a decision. Wonder how he ever got into the forecasting department!"

Fred and Annabelle talk over their problem and decide on a course of action to get the information they need before there can be any impact on their schedules. Annabelle will complete her report and, for the forecast numbers, simply fill in the numbers that were used during the proposal phase, even though they had been pulled out of the air by a salesman. Then Annabelle will ask each of her contacts at Floorshine, including Chuck, to read the draft before cleaning it up and sending it on to Floorshine top management as part of the biweekly progress report. They feel reasonably sure that Chuck will not allow bad numbers to go to the top—he will have to correct them. Annabelle will get her numbers, and Chuck won't lose face. If he decides that he still is unsure how long a piece of string is, Fred will get into the act and first meet with Chuck, and that failing, then with Chuck's manager.

As Annabelle found out, interviewing people to get the information needed is not always simple. Sometimes you end up having to nudge people; in the worst cases, you have to threaten, but you need to do everything you can to avoid getting to the threatening stage.

Interviewing should begin by assuring the customer that your company is there, under contract, to help solve some problem, but that it cannot be done without his help. Let the customer know you're completely dependent on him to supply you with information about his current operations and his ideas about the proposed new operations. As you go along, getting the customer to educate you, you in turn must educate him. He may not know anything about computers and programs. You can get him on your side and get a lot more help from him if you trade information rather than just drain him dry. As he learns more about what computers can do for him, he'll be more enthusiastic about giving you his time. Don't forget, some of the individuals you talk to may be disinterested, or uninterested, or even negative about what it is your company proposes to do. Your data-gathering interviews can be, for them, a big pain.

Make sure that you're talking to the right people—maybe Chuck is the wrong contact. Find out who would be better and get to that person. Do it diplomatically; avoid stepping on toes. One grumbler can do a lot to sabotage your work. One of the "right people" you *must* talk to is the *user*. The user is that part of the customer's organization who will eventually have to deal intimately with the product you deliver. Insist on talking to the user, even if customer management is reluctant to have you do so. It's easy enough for him to say, "Oh, don't worry. The guys in the parts inventory department are gonna love this system when we get it to them!" But the reality is, people who have no say in the new tools they're being handed very often balk at using them. First, people resist changing from the comfortable ways they're used to; second, people resent not being asked their opinions about changes that may vitally affect them.

It's a good idea to use some sort of interview form to aid in your data gathering. The form should state a few obvious items, such as the names of the interviewers and interviewees and the date. It should state the broad subject and then list specific numbered questions for discussion. As soon as possible after the interview, immediately if possible, the answers to the queries should be written out roughly and shown or read back to the interviewee to check on accuracy. Always summarize and play it back. Always end a particular portion of each interview with "Now, is this what you said?"

Participating

If you are building something for this customer that replaces an existing system (a manual operation, for example), have your analyst walked through the existing system. It's a lot easier to think about changing something if you first understand the something you are about to change. Let's say you're building an automated system for a company that sells books by mail order. Their present system is entirely manual. Your analyst can profitably spend at least a couple of days sitting in at each of the workstations in the current system observing, and where possible, assisting in the operations at that station: receiving and sorting incoming orders, matching orders against inventory, credit-checking the book customer, updating the mailing list, filling the order, invoicing, and so on. Imagine the benefits of experiencing the problems of the users of the old system if you're responsible for specifying the new. If a picture is worth a thousand words, participation is worth ten thousand.

There's a benefit beyond merely learning what goes on: This is a wonderful opportunity to snuggle up to the users. Participating with them in their various tasks and doing so in a way that plainly says: I'm dumb about your system, please teach me—that can do more than anything else to get their cooperation. It's a perfect time to begin planting ideas about what a new, computerized system might do to make their jobs easier. Just be careful not to give the impression that you're working on a system that will make their jobs obsolete.

WRITING IT DOWN

Keep in mind that the problem specification (also called the requirements specification, target specification, or system specification) is the foundation on which a system is to be built. It's not just some reference document that may or may not be used. The project's designers should be able, theoretically, to lay out a system based on the problem specification alone.

That's the goal, and the fact that the torpedo may zigzag a bit on the way to the goal does not diminish the importance of that goal. A quality problem specification does not guarantee project success, but a rotten one almost guarantees failure.[1]

The writing should be as short as possible, while leaving nothing out. Programmers delight in little contests to shave one more instruction from a program; analysts should likewise shave every unnecessary page from their product. Their success as analysts is inversely proportional to the weight of their documents. Why do you think book stores sell many more skinny novels than they do *War and Peace?* Don't think that the customer is impressed by tonnage. He'll be impressed by what answers his questions clearly while straining his brain the least.

The tone of the document should be such that it's comfortable reading for the customer—he should feel as though it's just about what he would have written. However, the analyst also needs to remember the designers. Their translation of the problem specification into design specifications should be smooth. You must search for and adopt current analysis methods that ease the translation process.

There are many types of analysis and documentation tools, none of them perfect. There is steady movement, however, away from reliance on old-style flowcharts plus narrative and toward more structured pictorial schemes. It is far from the purpose of this book to present particular documenting systems, but there are in the literature many excellent books detailing these systems. The schemes of most interest[2] are those that are not merely documenting tools but entire systems aimed at both aiding the analyst to perform the analysis and easing the way into the design phase. Some of the various analysis tools are, of course, at odds with one another. Any company involved in software projects simply *must* invest time and money in learning the available methods and must make decisions about which to adopt.[3]

In writing the problem specification, make sure it's as modular as a well-constructed program system and for most of the same reasons: (a) it's easier to understand a complex subject divided into meaningful chunks; (b) modularity will assist in relating the requirements in this document to

[1]Tom DeMarco in his book *Structured Analysis and System Specification* (Prentice-Hall, Inc., Englewood Cliffs, NJ, 1979), puts it this way: "Computer system analysis is like child-rearing; you can do grievous damage, but you cannot ensure success."

[2]See, for example, works by DeMarco; Jackson; Gane and Sarson cited in the Reference section.

[3]A good place for committee action. Hotshot representatives drawn from all the company's projects can be assigned the task of studying the tools available and recommending those the company ought to adopt across project lines, as far as that is possible.

LOOK, WE'LL FINISH THE DAMN SPEC TOMORROW

Daumier, Phédre: "Mon Chere, mes javelots," Howard P. Vincent Collection.

a later battery of tests intended to verify that those requirements have been met; (c) the document will need to be modified eventually.

It's alleged that salespeople in this business sometimes paint a picture with a very broad brush and leave it to others to handle the details. That won't do for the analyst. The analyst must write documents describing the customer's problem in descending levels of detail. I find it very frustrating to follow any discussion that immediately jumps into details. My brain doesn't work that way, and I don't think other people's operate much differently. In the Floorshine case, a problem specification ought to look roughly like this:

- What business is Floorshine in?
- What is Floorshine's organization? Name names and describe responsibilities.
- How big is Floorshine?
- How does Floorshine operate now? Trace the product from initial conception through design and manufacture to distribution and sales.
- How does Floorshine want to operate in the future? What parts of its operations are to be changed? What parts are *not* to be changed?

The last section must describe in detail just what it is that Floorshine expects you to do for them. It's the heart of the document, of course, but it will only be effective if the preceding topics are dealt with first. Don't jump into a document and say "Here are the changes" without first establishing what it is that's being changed.

Watch out for loss of consistency from one section to the next. This is especially hazardous when more than one analyst is writing the document (and that is most often the case). Consistency in organization and writing style makes any technical writing easier to follow, easier to use. Don't allow one section to be developed using, say, DeMarco's structured analysis, and another using some other method. Avoid having your document look like a sign I saw in a Louisiana store window: "Snake-bite kits and fried chicken." The two items on the sign just did not hang well together.

Make sure that no assumptions are left unwritten. Beware of winking Willie. The specification needs to cover everything that is to be included in the system; it also needs to state constraints or items *not* to be included. Now, it's obviously not possible to include in a specification *everything* that the system won't do, but there usually will be some items that perhaps have been contested by the customer, and you'll need to decide whether to include those negatives in order to head off future misunderstandings.

I read a newspaper article recently concerning the FDA. "This," said the article, "is clearly a gray area." Avoid gray areas in a problem specification. If you come to a section where you find yourself fudging or unable to write what that section promises, recognize that your analysis is not finished. If you can't write it clearly now, what are the designers going to do with that section when it's their turn? Sometimes we reach an impasse because we have a big sack of information and it does not seem to make sense. Organizing it may bring clarity. Kepner and Tregoe[4] make the point that organizing your information (into grids, decision tables, charts) may be the only way of arriving at valid conclusions.

AND IN YOUR SPARE TIME

I'm writing this book using a popular personal computer and a popular word-processing program. They're like my new Ford—nice when they work. But it's clear that two documents were shortchanged by the people who developed both the computer and the software.

First were the user manuals. When I began using my new system, I made many long-distance calls to some pleasant folks in Utah and lots of

---

[4]Kepner and Tregoe, *The Rational Manager*, McGraw-Hill, 1965.

calls to my local computer salesman. Some things in the manuals are stated obliquely, and some are flat-out wrong. The manual for the operating system, in particular, has obviously gone through many revisions and in the haste to get it to the market a lot of slop has gotten through. The trouble with many manuals is that nobody ever defines their audiences. People try to make each manual all things to all people.

An analyst should either write or have direct influence over the writing of user manuals.[5] While toiling over the problem specification, he or she should always have the user's interests in mind and should approach each piece of analysis with the question: Now, how would I explain this to a user? After all, the analyst describes *what* the system is supposed to do; he or she, then, is in the right frame of mind to explain to a user *what* the system does. The user also needs to know *how* the system can be made to do what it does, but not the *internal how* that a designer or programmer might offer. The user wants to know how to manipulate the system without getting involved with the jargon of the system's builders. My manuals read as though written by programmers whose primary concern was to get the boring job done and get back to writing programs.

The second document critical to the success of your system is one that defines acceptance criteria.[6] The initial phase of the project, when analysts are defining what the system is supposed to do, is the time for writing these criteria which, during the acceptance phase, will be used to determine whether your system actually satisfies the contract. Like lots of other things, acceptance criteria should be defined in the contract, but they're often expressed there so broadly as to be useless. Had meaningful acceptance criteria been written and met for my computer's software, I would not have to gnash my teeth as the system nosedives into an endless loop or fruitless disk search. One watches the little red disk drive light stay on without any error indication on the screen and one tries to break into the system without success. Well, I've been a programmer and I know these things happen. Systems crash and it's hard to get a handle on all the possible ways a crash may occur. But how about the software that detects an operator's error and is clearly in a position to display the error, but is too lazy to do so? In my system, if you have neglected to turn on the printer you want to use, a detectable condition, the programs simply ignore your request to print rather than tell you how you goofed and wait for you to switch on printer power. An acceptance criterion for this system might have been: Operator must be visually informed whenever the system detects an operator error.

---

[5]Some people insist that only the user can write the user manuals. This would be optimum. Many contracts, however, require the contractor to write them. In those cases, I think the analyst, with plenty of input from the user, is the appropriate writer.

[6]See Metzger, *Managing a Programming Project*.

KEEPING SOLUTIONS IN MIND

The analyst's job is to concentrate on *what* the system is to do, not *how* it is to be built, and the resulting document must stick to that premise. But let's be realistic—while thinking about the problem, you're bound to consider solutions. Not only is it impossible to compartmentalize your brain so thoroughly as to keep out design ideas, but it would be foolish to do so. One of the attributes of a good analyst is that he or she is also a good designer and programmer, or at least knows enough about designing and writing programs to understand what's reasonable and practicable. The analyst must understand the problems of converting the analysis document into programs if the analysis document is to be of the real world. It's entirely possible to write the *what* in such a way as to make the *how* difficult, if not impossible.

So what to do? Concentrate on the problem, don't ignore the solution. That's obvious. But generally avoid bending the analysis document to favor the programs; almost always go the other way and favor the user. Always keep in mind the customer's business objectives, because if the system you deliver does not satisfy those objectives, no matter how elegant a system it is, it's useless.

The analyst may be destined to go on to the next phase, change hats, and—presto!—become a designer. That's common and often practical, especially on smaller projects. Yet he or she *first* must wear the analyst's hat. The urge to get into the solution often is irresistible, but understand what DeBono[7] says about this: "Precise statement of a problem is a long step toward solving the problem."

GETTING IT APPROVED

Some of us like to work in isolation and only emerge from our caves after we have a finished product. An isolationist analyst might just as well commit suicide and spare everyone a lot of grief. You cannot expect to spend time data gathering, disappear into your office for a couple of months, and emerge with a product that has much chance of approval. The problem specification has got to be approved in the same way as the program system itself is approved—incrementally. Aim to make final approval a formality. When the customer sits down to read your final document, give him no surprises. Try to bore him.

Get approval of each new chunk by having the customer sign a simple approval form, but make sure the form makes clear the importance of

[7]Edward DeBono, *The Five-Day Course in Thinking*, Basic Books, 1967.

55

the approval. Try to avoid having busy people rubber-stamp things, thinking they'll be able to get another shot at it later. Do your best to point out the significance of each sign-off as it occurs. Ask the customer to use blood, not ink.

When you finish analysis and have a document all cleaned up and ready for final approval, conduct an oral review for the customer as well as contractor managers and lead technical people. Once the final fixes have been made, you finally have the first important *baseline* for the project. Hallelujah! But what is a baseline? It's an agreed-upon point of departure for everything that follows. It's something you'll constantly look back to in later phases for guidance. And it's something subject to change only under clear change-control procedures.[8] We often speak of "freezing" a baseline, but that term is misleading. It's frozen in the sense that no changes are allowed without contractor and customer invoking a predetermined set of change procedures. Never, *ever*, *EVER* allow changes to a baseline on a casual basis. As soon as that happens, you lose control of the project!

SO, WHAT *IS* AN ANALYST?

I recall with a shudder a session with a customer that almost lost us a job. There were a half-dozen or so of us from IBM and a like number from the customer's organization. We were discussing the customer's role in staffing a project. The customer in this case was supposed to program part of the job, and we were doing the rest. One of our bunch, an analyst we'll call Neander, had a high opinion of himself. I didn't share in the opinion, but Neander had our leader convinced he was indispensable.

We sat around a table and discussed who was to work on what; one of our guys would do module *x*, one of theirs would do module *y*. Then the leader of the customer delegation asked, "How do you feel about female programmers?" This was well before the fresh air of the equal rights movement. Most of us didn't really understand the question. Neander did.

"I despise them," he offered.

Now, you might argue that there is a place for Neander somewhere on a project. Just keep him out of sight and don't put him in the same office with a woman. I would argue that there is *no* place for him, out of sight or not. We've come a long way, Neander.

I don't mean to wave my ERA flag here. The question posed by the customer might just as well have been, "What do you think of cus-

---

[8]See change control in Metzger, *Managing a Programming Project*, and in Robert L. Glass, *Modern Programming Practices*, Prentice-Hall, Inc., Englewood Cliffs, N.J., 1982.

tomers?'' and Neander might just as well have answered, ''I despise them,'' as I believe he did. Why tolerate someone such as Neander in a position vis-à-vis the customer?[9]

An analyst does not have to be Secretary of State. I don't think it takes special training or a rare talent to produce an analyst who can relate well to people. It simply takes a decent human being who likes other human beings and does not carry around a lot of heavy baggage in the form of anger and prejudice. Part of the analyst's job is to get busy people to give information. As a manager, you need to choose people as analysts who are able to be friendly and businesslike at the same time.

An analyst must enjoy providing a service to a customer. Other project people, such as programmers, are more removed from the customer and are only indirectly providing a service. However, the analyst, like a clerk in a store, actually faces the customer, talks to him, tries to answer his or her needs—and to be good, the analyst must *like* the idea of being of service. I go out of my way to compliment those rare people I encounter in stores who handle my needs cheerfully, politely, and with knowledge. Any customer appreciates someone who deals with him or her in a professional, courteous manner. It's important that a manager, as part of the early training of an analyst, instill the idea of service. It's very easy for a manager to set the wrong tone by referring to the customer in derogatory or condescending terms, and it would be the rare analyst who did not carry that negativism into meetings with the customer. I'm not suggesting, of course, that all customers are equally lovable, but only that you need to start out as though they are.

Your analyst must be technically competent. People end up in jobs for various reasons, not all of them sane. I've known ''analysts'' who were very poor technicians, appointed because they had been good salespeople or simply because they were available and, what the heck, anyone can be an analyst! Earlier I talked about the idea of keeping solutions in mind even while formulating the problem. Analysts need a good technical background if they are to avoid committing the project to the unattainable.

There are many things an analyst ought to be, but no one is born an analyst. One of management's most important functions is to train people for their jobs. Fred Freud seems to be training Annabelle by throwing her at a job and fixing problems as they arise. That's not good enough. There ought to be formal training within the company for analysts, just as there

[9]After reviewing this section, Ray Klaskin asked: "Who in his right mind would put someone of that temperament in front of a customer?" Good question. People like Roy, who *is* in his right mind, would not tolerate Neander vis-à-vis the customer. Others would . . . and did!

normally is for programmers and security guards. Training topics should include:

- Current analysis methods[10]
- Interviewing
- Effective writing
- Effective presentation
- Software engineering economics[11]
- Estimating techniques[12]

I have not included data processing training in this list because I think it should be a prerequisite for becoming an analyst in the first place. Training in programming does not mean, however, that the analyst must have been a programmer before becoming an analyst—only that he or she understand programming very well. Some managers feel strongly, in fact, that programmers and designers make poor analysts because they are incapable of separating problem solutions from problem descriptions. If you have an analyst who, like Annabelle, immediately jumps to solutions, you have at least a retraining problem. In the worst cases, you'll find you have a bad match and you'll have to rethink your job assignments.

MANAGING ANNABELLE

Fred Freud wearily plops himself in a chair across the desk from his boss, Peter Projectmanager.

"Cripes!" he sighs. "What a day!"

Peter Projectmanager smiles wanly and nods in agreement. Yes, it *had* been a tough day. He looks across at his analysis manager and laughs: "Take off your Floorshines, Fred, and relax."

Fred glances at his feet and grimaces. "Peter," he begins, "I learned a lot today. Old Bootfoot was really ticked off . . ." Bootfoot is the project manager at Floorshine. "I'm sorry you had to witness that . . ."

"Me, too, Fred. But we can pick up the pieces and still do a good job here. I've got some thoughts, but I'd like to hear yours."

Fred studies his hands and practices making his thumbs circle one another. Then he sits up straighter and leans forward.

---

[10]Such as those proposed by DeMarco, Gane and Sarson, Jackson.

[11]See Barry W. Boehm, *Software Engineering Economics*, Prentice-Hall, Inc., Englewood Cliffs, N.J., 1981.

[12]See Aron, DeMarco, Boehm, and Biggs et al.

"Look, Peter, let's first understand this before we go on: I don't blame anybody but myself. Not Annabelle, not Chuck or Sneakers, not Willie Wink."

"There's lots of blame to go around, Fred. I'm not exactly pure, either!"

"Well, to start off with, I made the mistake of assuming this was a pretty straightforward job and I felt safe enough putting Annabelle on it. Sometimes you figure somebody really bright can handle anything that comes up . . . "

"Mmmmm. No way. A talented salesman can make a rotten programmer."

"Yeah! Speaking of salesmen . . . will the company really be committed to supplying the utility programs Willie promised Floorshine, even though there's nothing in the contract about it?"

"Maybe not legally, but morally . . . ?" Peter shrugs and spreads his palms in a gesture that says "Who knows?" After a moment of reflection, Peter continues: "I think we're going to have to honor his promises or else look pretty bad. Our immediate problem, though, is their rejection of our problem spec."

"Yeah," Fred says, "their list of objections is pretty long, but we should be able to satisfy them with a couple of weeks of rework. I knew we should have bypassed that damned Chuck . . . the forecast data we finally got out of him were so fattened up that they threw all the rest of our thinking out of whack."

"True, but just think how bad off we'd be if their management hadn't finally caught the bad info. If we'd gotten into design still working with those fat numbers, we'd have ended up specifying a system big enough to run the Pentagon, let alone Floorshine!"

"Mmmmm! Chuck was really trying to cover his butt! Couple weeks back I should have seen that coming. Instead of being afraid of hurting his feelings or alienating him, I should have gone straight to his management."

"In hindsight, that's true. We all need to be a little firmer in dealing with the customer. I think, Fred, we need to be firmer in dealing with our own people too."

Fred feels his neck and face warming.

"For instance, later today Willie Wink will be coming by and I'm going to read him the riot act. His under-the-counter promises are gonna cost us plenty. But, as far as the problem spec is concerned, it's you and me and Annabelle we need to concentrate on."

"Well," Fred breaks in, "I think I understand my mistakes there. I was too busy to stay close to what she was doing. She was new to this job and I left her too much on her own. Didn't train her . . . I should at least have worked with her for a few days till I could be sure she was on track. But what I really should have done was team her up with somebody experienced. I don't think, after this, I'd ever make one person alone responsible for analysis, no matter what the job.''

''We keep learning, don't we?'' Peter interrupts. He likes what he hears Fred saying. ''It wasn't too many years ago we might have skipped analysis altogether and gone right into design!''

''Or programming!'' Fred adds.

The two talk about how to repair the damage already done and how to avoid more of the same. They consider how to revise the project schedule, since the problem specification will now be about a month late. They part late in the afternoon. Fred seeks out Annabelle to get her restarted, with another analyst to assist her. With some queasiness, Peter ponders the new schedule they had roughed out.

''Can't cut short the design phase,'' he mutters. Score a point for Peter. ''We'll have to trim back on system test!'' Subtract two points from Peter.

It's five o'clock and time to go home. Peter Projectmanager puts on his jacket, picks up his faithful briefcase, and starts for the door. He literally bumps into a somber Fred Freud.

''Hi, Fred! Talk to Annabelle about the rework?''

''Yup!''

''And about teaming up with someone?''

''Yup!''

''Go okay?''

''Nope!''

Peter sighs. ''What's the problem?''

''Annabelle has quit the company.''

There's an old saying in the painting racket, generally attributed to Rembrandt: If you would paint an apple, first *be* an apple. In the good old days, anyone could manage anything. If you need someone to manage an analysis group, well—there's Fred over by the water cooler. He's not real busy—he's our man. Hey, Fred . . .

However, the good old days are littered with failed projects, and we're trying to do better. We cannot be satisfied with a project landscape resembling a scene from *Road Warrior*.

If you're going to manage analysts, there are some things you need to do about your own credentials. Get yourself trained in the current thinking about doing analysis. Just as programmers are breaking free from the old days of ragged flowcharts, sloppy coding, and wasteful debugging techniques, analysts, too, are seeing new tools and methods being advanced and tried. More structured and disciplined approaches are slowly replacing the old. If you came to manage the analysis group straight from managing, say, programmers, you're in the same boat as Annabelle. You have a new discipline to learn, and some other things to unlearn. Is there a modern course for analysts in your company? If so, take it; if not, get one started. If you're in charge of analysts, you're in the business of building foundations; everything that follows you in the project will rest on your work. Don't begin blindly.

If your first duty as an analysis manager is to get yourself trained, certainly next in importance is to train your analysts. Fred Freud got Annabelle off to a shaky start because he failed to *re*train her as an analyst. Her whole inclination was to do what she was comfortable doing, solving problems. Freud gets an "F" in training. (In fairness, though, he did at least recognize that she was doing the wrong job, and he attempted to redirect her.)

He also flubbed in sending Annabelle off as the sole analyst on the job. Even had she received proper training, it was not a good idea to let her handle her first assignment alone. In fact, I don't believe any job of any size should be staffed by a single analyst. There should be at least two people, so that one can always ask the other: Is this what you understood the customer to say? This is a case where I think it's better to use two people for a month than one person for two months. When the job is so small that there is no way to justify more than one person doing the analysis, the manager can at least spend the first couple of days on the project with the analyst to help assure a sound start.

When it became necessary to circumvent Chuck and find someone to talk to who really was in charge, it was Annabelle's job, as analyst, to do the circumventing. However, given someone as inexperienced as she, the manager should step in. Fred could have called on his counterpart in the Floorshine business and established who else, besides Chuck, was in a position to get Annabelle the information she needed.

The Leaning Tower of Pisa, Courtesy Bob Sparks.

The Designer

Chapter 3

One day back in the sixties, I had a possum in my attic. I had a typical ranch house whose roof overhung the outside walls. The possum had settled himself snugly back in part of the overhang where I could see him in the flashlight beam, but I couldn't crawl close enough in the restricted attic space to get hold of him. I analyzed the problem: The job requirements were to get the bugger out without hurting him and to do so without getting bitten.

I had other things to do, so I jumped on the first solution that came into my head. I'm embarrassed to tell you that I began removing the plywood panels outside the house that formed the underside of the overhang near where the brute was settled. Off came the first panel, not without plenty of sweat and not without messing up the panel where the nails pulled through. Naturally, when the panel came off Mr. Possum was nowhere to be seen. Being considerably smarter than his antagonist, he simply moved to an adjacent panel. I had not designed a good solution for my problem. I could have removed all of the panels from the overhang around the entire house and still would have been no closer to my prey. All he needed to do was keep moving about the attic and I'd never catch him. And even if I did, I'd have to rebuild half my house when all was done.

I looked at my young kids watching me and decided I'd better find a simpler solution or all my credibility as a parent would be shot. I came down from the ladder and announced that I would now do my Marlin Perkins bit and capture this beast with a snare. I rigged a loop in a piece of rope at the end of a long bamboo pole and crawled back into the attic. In the flashlight beam, I found Mr. Possum in the overhang a few feet from where I had torn loose the first piece of panel. He sat calmly looking at me and probably wondering what in hell I would tear apart next. This time, I had him. My superior intellect (superior to the possum's, that is), knowing that possums really do "play possum," had convinced me he would stay still while I poked the long pole toward him, slipped the noose around his neck and pulled it snug. He did and I did, and pretty soon I had gently tugged him out of the overhang and near enough to me that I could steer him into a bucket, release the noose, and put a lid on the bucket to keep him in there until I could crawl down out of the attic and display my catch to my kids. We transferred the possum to a garbage can and took a ride into some woods, where we set him free.

Two minutes spent thinking about the problem would have produced the better solution without the silliness of tearing the house apart, and that better solution would have saved me the considerable work involved in repairing the overhang. It also would have allowed me to save face with my kids. I'm sure they were smart enough to see that my house-wrecking was dumb (although they were also smart enough not to point it out to me).

I'm not the only impatient fellow around. People are always implementing half-baked solutions to problems. Programming types are notorious for this, and lots of programming managers and plenty of customers are so anxious to see something abuilding that they allow, or even promote, coding before a solid design has been thought out. That's always wrong. Always. ALWAYS.

Can you imagine pouring concrete, laying bricks, and erecting girders for a building that has not yet been blueprinted, and then later tearing out the girders and chopping away the bricks to fix things? If it's wrong to build physical objects before designing them, why isn't it wrong to build programs before designing them? Because program instructions are intangible and easily changed? No way! It's relatively just as expensive to toss out badly conceived program bricks as it is to chop out building bricks. If you are a design manager, get the job done right. Don't have programming managers later screaming at you for passing on bad design.

BRIDGING THE MUCK

A designer's job is to build a solid bridge between the analysts and the programmers. The analyst's output is the designer's input. The designer's output is the programmer's input. The designer must translate the analyst's *what* documents (usually called problem specifications or requirements specifications) into *how* documents (which I call design specifications). The design specification should be a natural extension of the problem specification. If you have chosen your documenting tools well, a reader will make the transition from one document to the next without trauma.

Since a well-written problem specification may contain some implied design and may even *look* like a design document, and since everyone is always anxious to get on with the coding, there may be a temptation to skip design as a formal phase and begin writing code, designing as you go. There may come a time when no book need talk ever again about this problem; there may come a time when everyone understands that it's necessary to design before coding. But not yet. People still jump from some half-baked understanding of the problem right into coding a solution. The design bridge never gets built and lots of programmers and managers fall into the dark slime below. You can see their little pointy heads bobbing up and down as they disappear into the distance. Good riddance.

Whatever the cost of designing well, the cost of *not* designing well is many times greater. Here's a common scenario: On a typical project, a design has been rushed through and an impressive list of about fifty modules has been identified and strung together neatly enough to convince an uneducated management that the design is complete and programming may now begin. The designers know that the interface mechanisms have not been thoroughly worked out and they know that one black-box module is going to be tricky, but Tricky Dick Programmer, who also played the role of one of the designers, knows pretty much how he's going to handle it. Two months go by and tons of code pile up in the master listings, enough to make any programming manager proud. Integration test begins. Programmers find it necessary to establish ad hoc interfacing conventions as they go along. Intermodule communication becomes confused, integration attempts fail, Rolaids stock becomes a good buy. Tricky Dick gets an offer to work for the Republican National Committee and he leaves the project.

A lot of time is lost as attempts are made to resolve the communication problems, but there have been so many private arrangements made that by now there is a hopeless mishmash of modules that are anything but independent. The fixes have involved poor module coupling and a load of pathological connections.[1] Tricky Dick's modules, especially the one that was a question mark even to him, are indecipherable. It finally becomes clear even to management that all motion is in reverse.

Managers are shuffled, speeches are made, overtime is authorized, unlimited computer time is made available. Just about everything is done *except* to stop and redesign. I've seen it happen, and you probably have too unless you're new to this business. By rushing through design, *n* weeks were saved. Then many times *n* weeks are lost trying to fix things. However, calendar time is perhaps the least of the problems. People exhaust themselves physically trying to make things work; they exhaust themselves emotionally knowing they're producing garbage; costs go through the roof; the customer becomes a harsh, demanding enemy rather than an understanding partner; morale sinks out of sight; and if a product finally is delivered, it's a patchwork that is bound to fail as soon as it's subjected to real conditions not envisioned during the frantic testing.

The cost of not designing properly can only be measured according to some sort of escalating scale. There is not a simple, one-to-one relationship between a design flaw and its consequences. If the building is partly

[1]See Edward Yourdon and Larry L. Constantine, *Structured Design: Fundamentals of a Discipline of Computer Program and Systems Design*, Prentice-Hall, Inc., Englewood Cliffs, N.J., 1978.

up and you have to move an elevator shaft six feet to the left, the cost of moving it will dwarf the cost of having designed it right in the first place. Design errors ripple through everything that follows. Says Lawrence Peters: " . . . the design errors in a system are the most persistent and costly ones with which to contend."[2]

As a design manager, you've got to understand the difference between good and poor design and you've got to subject your design to scrutiny by other designers, as well as programmers, analysts, and the customer. Before you even begin to design, you must understand and choose the tools you'll use.

FIRST THINGS FIRST

It's the first day of the design phase on Project SOW. The manager of the design group, Marty Martinet, has gathered his designers for a kickoff meeting.

"Good morning!" he bellows as he comes bounding into the room. His ruddy face glows with good cheer.

"Good morning," mumble the five designers sitting about the table.

"Dennis, glad you could join us," says Marty to one of the group. Dennis is a senior designer on loan from one of the other projects here at Super Software, Inc. It seems the Floorshine project has been delayed and Dennis is available.

Marty cracks his knuckles loudly. Still standing before the seated designers, he takes a stack of papers from his briefcase and passes them around the table.

"Here's the problem spec for the job," he says. "Copy for each of you. I looked at it over the weekend . . . looks pretty good. And on time, too! That's a first!" The five designers begin leafing through their copies of the problem specification. After a few minutes, Marty goes on:

"I'd like you to take today to read through the spec. Then first thing tomorrow morning we'll meet again right here and talk about the schedule and who'll do what. Okay?"

Dennis speaks up: "Will we be using HIPO?"

Marty looks at him quizzically. "HIPO?"

"Or do you guys use structure charts over here? We've tried them both in our department and we're getting the hang of using them."

The other four designers shuffle their feet under the table and glance toward Marty, whose face has taken on the benevolent look of a kindly dictator. He walks around the table and stands alongside Dennis. With a hand on Dennis' shoulder, he says: "We stick with the tried-and-true here,

[2]L. J. Peters, *Software Design: Methods and Techniques*, Yourdon Press, N.Y., 1981.

Dennis. Good old flowcharts! We've had lots of discussions about the so-called structured techniques among the group here . . . '' he glances at his four designers who sit looking on impassively, " . . . and we've decided they are all just fancied-up ways of doing what can be done simply with flowcharts." He pats Dennis on the shoulder and marches around to the front of the table and leans forward, knuckles on the table. His voice slowly rises in pitch. "Back when I worked on SAGE . . . " His four programmers stiffen and try not to make eye contact with one another. " . . . we had nothing to use but flowcharts and they worked great. You take practically any programmer and start talking about a programming problem and what's the first thing he does? Scribbles a flowchart on whatever's handy, that's what!" Dennis is beginning to inch back in his chair as Marty leans more forward and his knuckles whiten as they sustain his weight against the conference table.

"Trouble is, all these guys . . . Mills and Yourdon and the whole bunch . . . they sit in their ivory towers and dream up complicated ways to do what we already know how to do with good old flowcharts!" Marty's face is three shades redder than normal. He takes a deep breath, pulls back, and composes himself. His voice lowers to a more paternalistic tone and he smiles down at Dennis. "No, Dennis, none of that for us. Flowcharts it is . . . besides, if we messed around with a different system, we'd never make the schedule. Take too long to learn."

Somewhere in the past, Marty Martinet stopped growing. It happens to lots of people. Advancing technology catches up with them and they run out of steam and let technology pass them by. As a manager, you may be frustrated by the demands on your time, but you've got to make room for your continuing education. And as an educated manager, you'll understand that designers and their managers need to choose thoughtfully their design methodology—the rules, procedures, and tools to be used during the design process.

There once was little choice; designers simply drew up flowcharts, threw in some narrative and a few supporting tables, and that was it. Now you get to choose from among a menu of methodologies. You may protest that such choices should have been made long before the design phase arrived, and you would be right. As I said in Chapter 1, the designers should already know how they're going to go about designing before it's time to design. If no conscious decisions have been made to use this methodology or that, management has been asleep. You can't expect to retrain your designers in a day to get them using structured design if they've been using nothing but flowcharts all during their careers. It's probably better in that case to go along with whatever methods your designers are used to and swear to change things before the next project.

GETTING AT THE POSSUM

Armed with a proper set of design tools, your next concern is to understand thoroughly the problem the analysts have passed on to your designers and the constraints under which they must work. But then what? Is there some reliable, automatic means of arriving at a decent design?

There is not. Tools and an understanding of the problem can take you to the edge of battle, but then you're on your own. The guidelines suggested by structured design techniques will help steer you, but the real work of design is a mental process that relies on experience and ingenuity. Fortunately, you can seek out designers who possess both of those qualities, especially experience. There are very few program systems built that are *really* new. Try to name a type of program that has not been written before. If just one of Marty Martinet's designers have had previous experience in a project similar to SOW, that's a huge advantage. If *all* of his designers have had similar experience on a related system, that might not be so hot. While it's obviously helpful to be able to draw on past experience, it's dangerous for everyone to have that *same type of background* because there may be too little questioning of the way it was done before. If SOW is a payroll system and all five of Marty's people are payroll experts, where will fresh ideas and new approaches come from? Who will act as devil's advocate? Who will put forth a fresh, new approach[3] because he or she doesn't know any better? Look at Marty . . . he's so hidebound that he can't give up his precious flowcharts. You need people with related experience as your designers, but you need people with *un*related experience to keep the others from plodding along the same old rutted road.

Allow for detours and dead ends during design. Each approach thrown out narrows the choices so that you get ever closer to an acceptable answer. Notice I said *acceptable*; don't worry about finding that ultimate, perfect solution. You usually can't afford the time for such a search. This is one of the times that a manager, even if not deeply involved in the day-to-day design process, must exercise leadership. If you're the design manager, you need to keep one eye on the current design scheme your people are proposing and the other on your schedule. You need to be able to say this design is what you'll go with. Your designers may object that it's not elegant enough, but you need to make the determination that the design is sound and satisfies the requirements of the job, and that further iteration

---

[3]There is a winding river in Tennessee that is crossed by an interstate highway six times along a stretch of just a few miles. Imagine the cost of six three-lane interstate highway bridges! I always wonder whether a cheaper approach might have been to straighten out the river.

would not be economically justified. That last mouthful is what excellence in managing designers is all about: *Is the design sound? Does it satisfy the job requirements? Would further expenditure of resources be justified?* Tearing the house down to get the possum out would clearly not be sound; shooting him would violate the humaneness clause in the job requirements spec; and training a lady possum to woo him down from the attic would involve unjustifiable time and expense.

WHAT IS GOOD DESIGN?

How do you know that your designers have come up with a good design? There's some decent guidance in the literature, but one of your best assurances that a design is good is when good designers *say* it is. If you have a design reviewed by competent people who did not produce the design, that may be your best way of knowing the quality of the work. Structured walkthroughs are an excellent means of assessing design quality. Among those who participate in such reviews should be the people who are to inherit the design specifications—the lead programmers and their managers who are to produce the programs based on your design. If you're a

A STRUCTURED WALKTHROUGH

Bruegel, "Parable of the Blind," The National Museum, Naples.

small operation and the same people who design end up doing the programming as well, it's imperative to find experienced, competent reviewers from outside your immediate group who have no stake in the outcome.

You can do much more. You can provide training for yourself and your designers. Since the late 1970s, a great deal of excellent work has been done by people on the trail of better design methods and tools.[4] The books and articles written by these researchers are a good place to start. Many of the authors offer seminars and courses on design, and they can be reached through their publishers. I constantly nag you to look for ways to educate yourself and understand the newest methodologies because I know how easy it is to fall behind. In my early years as a programmer and as a manager, I did not take advantage of what instruction was available (always too busy with today's problems), and I paid for that. Catching up is always tougher than keeping up.

A BRIDGE TOO FAR?

"This is all very well, Mr. Nickleby, and very proper, so far as it goes . . . but it doesn't go far enough." So says a Dickens character in *Nicholas Nickleby*.

"This design stinks, boss! It makes me nothing but a coder! It goes too far!" So says Perry Programmer of the design specification just handed over by the design group.

Somewhere in between those extremes is the limit to which an overall design should be carried. The programmers who inherit the design need latitude to invent solutions; they don't want to supply code like so many robots. Give them a chance to contribute something of excellence. Don't have architects putting bricks in place—even if they're good at it. Let the bricklayers do it. It's what they're paid for and they are good at it.

Another reason for stopping overall design short of a mass of detail: You need a concise document for communicating with the customer and with your own management. I had a customer whose eyes not only glazed over, but actually nearly closed whenever I got beyond a certain level of detail. At about the third level of flowchart, he looked like a lizard going into a coma.

Finally, remember that this design document is a baseline,[5] and it must be kept manageable in size and content if it is to be a useful future reference point for change proposals.

---

[4] See the References section.

[5] See baselines and change procedures in Metzger.

THE CART BEFORE THE HORSE PUTTING

Project SOW is well along in the design phase. There are lots of charts, flowcharts done by Marty Martinet's four designers and structure charts done by Dennis. Marty is content to see the pile of charts growing and is sufficiently lulled by the briefings he gets from his designers that he is not too worried that they're not all using the same tools.

On Friday, he and his designers give a briefing to Paula Projectmistress and her staff. Paula is putting together the rest of the project organization that she will need to program, test, and install the system that Marty is designing.

The first twenty minutes of the review go smoothly enough, as the analysis manager discusses the SOW problem and Marty begins presenting the design. He plasters a wall with flowcharts, leads the group through the overview chart, then turns to his chief designer, Dicky, to go through the more detailed charts. Paula Projectmistress soon interrupts:

"Dicky, so far, so good. But I've been glancing ahead at your other charts, and all I see is programs . . . "

Dicky cocks his head questioningly.

"What I mean is," Paula continues, "I don't see anything representing the database. Do you have separate charts showing how you're handling that?"

"Well . . . " Dicky flushes a little and glances toward Marty. "We're working out the database as we go along. As we see the need for the next item of data, we add it on. We've got a chart showing all the tags and field lengths, but we didn't prepare it for the briefing."

Paula abruptly turns her questions toward Marty. "Isn't this pretty much a database-driven system? My understanding has always been—and I think our problem spec bears this out—that we're dealing with a rather large assemblage of fairly complex data with plenty of cross-referencing."

"That's true," answers Marty, not sure of what Paula is getting at.

"Then doesn't the arrangement of the database become pretty critical?"

"Well, data's data!" exclaims Marty reassuringly, with a shrug and a smile.

"Seems to me," continues Paula, getting a little restless, "that if you're dealing with a mess of FORTRAN calculations with only small amounts of data in and out, or if you're writing an assembler and processing a statement at a time, your database problems are not huge. But in SOW, where three-quarters of the programs manipulate the data, the structure of the database becomes at least as important as the structure of the programs, hmmmm?"

73

Dicky looks toward Marty for help, while Dennis sits inspecting his shoes. Dennis had argued for structuring the database early in the design effort, but had been brushed aside by Marty. Marty belches softly and looks for a way out:

"Paula, I think we have what you're looking for . . . we just don't have it ready for the briefing. Didn't think we'd bore you with a lot of details about the data."

Paula glances at her watch. "Suppose we continue the briefing Monday morning. I'd like to see the data structure charts right along with the program charts."

The meeting ends. Marty and his group make tracks for his office, while Paula takes the elevator to the next floor. She stops at Peter Projectmanager's door and sticks her head inside.

"Peter! Got a minute?"

Peter looks up from the papers on his desk and smiles: "Hi, Paula! C'mon in!"

She settles in a chair across from Peter.

"How'd your briefing go?" Peter asks cheerfully. Then, glancing at his watch, he adds: "Hmmmm! Pretty short briefing. Good or bad?" He is pretty sure he knows the answer.

"Listen . . . " Paula begins, "I've only been here a short time . . . you've been around longer. What do you think of Marty Martinet? Can he hack it?" Without waiting for an answer, she relates her misgivings about the handling of SOW's database. "I'm afraid what I'm going to see Monday is a collection of data fancied up to look like an honest-to-God structured database. Worse yet, I didn't see any real attempt at designing the overall system first, before either the programs or the database. What I'm really concerned about is, do I have the right person as a design manager?"

A week later, Marty Martinet has been reassigned to address a pressing problem in New Jersey. Dennis Designer has been promoted to design manager. He is meeting with the four SOW designers.

"This is all pretty brain-rattling," he begins. "An awful lot has happened this week. I hope you'll all bear with me while I get used to this job."

They chat a while until all five feel more comfortable, and then Dennis makes some announcements.

"Paula has arranged to reschedule the project by a few weeks," he says. "Here's what the new schedule looks like. It gives us a chance to get a fresh start, and since we already know plenty about the job, this time it'll go a lot faster. We're not going to switch tools, since you're all comfortable with flowcharts. We can't stop and retrain and hope to make the schedule. I'll be doing this section of the design and I'll use the same methods you're using. Right after this project, I have Paula's promise we can all attend a structured design course being offered in New York."

There are appreciative nods from the four designers.

"The main thing I want to stress right now," continues Dennis, "is that we'll be designing the database from scratch and we need to get its overall structure pretty solid before we get very far into the programs. But even before that, we need to *really* go back to the beginning and look at the overall system design. Now here's what I think we need to do . . . "

MANAGING DICKY

You manage designers pretty much like anyone else, but certain areas need special care.

Controlling Change

It's late in the day and Dicky comes barging into your office.

"They've changed the specs again!!" he cries.

"Who?"

"The customer!"

"What makes you think so?"

"Alfie said so. He just came back from there."

"Ask Alfie to come in, will you?"

It happens regularly on any job. No matter how careful you are about writing specifications and getting them signed off, there will be proposed changes. Some will eventually be accepted and some will not. You deal with changes by having clear change control procedures.[4] But you need to do more than simply *have* the procedures; once they're sold to the customer, you need to make sure your designers understand and abide by them. They need to understand always that the problem specification they are designing from never changes until they hear it from you (management). No matter how many informal discussions there may be about possible changes, your people must be trained never to agree to changes, but only to pass them on through your change control channels. If there is any place on a project where formal procedures must be adhered to, this is it.

Alfie comes in.

"Dicky says the customer wants something changed. What's it all about, Alfie?"

[4]See Metzger.

75

"They need the ident field expanded. They've just had a corporate directive to expand their product identifiers to eight characters."

"Have they written us a change request yet? I haven't seen one."

"Gee, I don't know."

"Okay, no problem. I'll call over there and make sure they put the thing in as a formal change request. If they do, and if it gets approved, it may have to wait for version 2 of the system."

Alfie is getting more relaxed now. "Do you want us to see what it would cost to make the change?"

"Nope! Business as usual until we get it in writing . . . or if it's something earth-shaking, I'll be around to let you know. In any case, always listen to their requests, but always tell them to get it in the change proposal mill."

Alfie leaves happy, and you do your management duty and get on the phone to make sure the change proposal, if it really is one, is being handled according to the procedures you and the customer agreed to. No fuss. No panic. All in a day's work. Ho-hum. Some things on a project ought to be boringly routine.

I've known some managers, one in particular whom I'll call Don, who insulate their subordinates too completely from the real world of change. Don was an excellent programmer and designer. However, as a *manager* of programmers and designers, Don became much like a rooster protecting his flock. That's probably better than the other extreme, the manager who filters out nothing and causes his people a lot of lost time and energy—yet Don does some real damage. The people who work for him are in for some shock when they finally waddle out of the warm nest and face the big, bad world. People who are *too* protected by their managers may be temporarily more efficient than others, but they'll eventually pay a price, like overprotected kids leaving Iowa and heading for New York.

Avoiding Wanderlust

Dicky is going to get the urge, sooner or later, to depart from the problem specification. He'll want to add some frills that are not called for in the spec. What he might not appreciate, and what you should, is that an addition that may cost the designer nothing more than a box on a chart is likely to cost a great deal more later on, in programming and testing the goody. It often will be reasonable to make some changes, but don't let that be Dicky's prerogative. Again, we're talking about controlling changes, but this time they're dreamed up by your people, not the customer. Treat them all the same: Control them.

How Much Design?

Constantly review the evolving design specification to be sure that every-thing in the problem specification is being satisfied—but satisfied to an *appropriate level.* Don't look for cookbooks to tell you what the appropriate level is: There are none. Simply do your best to heed these guidelines: (a) explicitly satisfy each requirement in the problem specification; (b) stop as far short of coding as possible; (c) explicitly define the rules for all com-munication among program modules, between programs and data, and between people and programs; and (d) don't leave problems to be resolved during programming whose solutions might cause changes in your base-line design. I probably should add: (e) aim for a perfect, change-free de-sign, but don't be surprised when you don't get it.

Keep the Customer Tuned In

Choose designers who can work well with the customer; don't hire Nean-der, who thinks customers are a pain. Although the analysts were in clos-est touch with the customer, your designers cannot ignore him. Your peo-ple, and you, must keep appropriate customer people apprised of your progress and your approaches. You need to answer questions as design proceeds and maintain customer confidence. You need to set the tone so that your people have a healthy attitude and don't consider the customer a bother. Obviously, you must also keep the customer from interfering with design progress: There's such a thing as too much togetherness, and it's up to you to establish how much is too much.

Training (Again)

If you let your people rot away under stacks of old flowcharts, they'll one day be ready for the compost heap. Whatever is being offered as a new technique, tool, or procedure, take a close enough look to be able to adopt it or ignore it intelligently. I've probably sounded so far as though I think flowcharts should be banned. I don't. I only insist that not looking at what else there is to offer is foolish.

Daumier, "Narcissus," Museum of Fine Arts, Boston.

The Programmer

Chapter 4

In 1955, I got my first real job. I was through with college, through with the Air Force, and not prepared for anything. IBM had built a new plant in Kingston, in upstate New York, near where I was raised. It was either IBM or the road gang, so I applied and was hired as a programmer. I had no idea what a programmer was or what computers were all about, but for ninety dollars a week I was about to find out.

After a few weeks' training, I joined the SAGE project. Through sheer luck, I was assigned, along with another rookie, to write a control program for the SAGE standby computer, one of the choicer assignments around. SAGE was an air-defense system whose computers were to be dotted around the country. Each SAGE site boasted two computers, one for active air defense, the other a standby, to be ready to go active if the other failed. The two computers occupied a huge concrete building: There were very large consoles, rows of tape drives, loads of vacuum tubes, miles of cabling and air conditioning ducts, and an extensive array of blinking lights and manual switches. Programs were entered either through balky card readers or reels of tape.

I feel sorry for any programmers today who do not get their hands on the computer (many do, of course, through satellite microcomputers or various forms of terminals). When my friends and I got computer time, it wasn't down the hall at three o'clock next Tuesday. It was in Ann Arbor or Kansas City, and we got the whole building, often both computers, for a twelve-hour shift. The only impediment between us and the computer was an assembly program and a card reader—no batch submissions, no operating system, no job control cards, no operator. The computer was ours.

The finest feature of the SAGE computer was its console with banks of lights telling you, in octal, the contents of any of various registers or memory locations, and a wonderful set of indicator lights and manual switches that allowed you positive control of almost every operation. You could flip program-sensed switches to direct programs toward different paths; watch lights to know which module of the program was currently operating (I don't think we used the word *module* then); alter memory locations from the console. Most wonderful of all were the single-step switches that allowed you to execute your program one instruction at a time. I can't tell you how many delightful hours we spent sitting at the console executing programs an instruction at a time, loops and all. I don't know how long it took us to devise better tracing methods than that, and if I knew I probably wouldn't tell you. I blush easily.

Those "good old days" *were* good in some ways. The programmer was not a slave to operating systems and language constraints and programming standards—those things were still in the future. We worked hard, if not smart, and nobody screamed too much when things were late or when budgets were exceeded. In fact, from our lowly vantage point, it seemed there were few budget constraints. A company that paid me ninety dollars a week couldn't be worried too much about budgets.

A few decades later, it's clear that the romance of the old days is not only gone for good, but ought to be. (I used to dream a lot of the days of chivalry and knights and castles. These days, I'm happy for central heating and indoor johns.) And yet, progress does cost us something. Placing operating systems and complicated procedures between the programmer and his computer may lessen the programmer's sense of involvement and caring, much the same as if a skilled machinist were separated from his lathe by some sort of intermediary and only allowed to deal with his lathe remotely. Today's use of terminals that allow programs and data to be entered from the programmer's desk allows the programmer to get back "in touch" with the computer.

Programmers from the first generation of computers often fell into sloppy habits. There was little discipline, few tools with which to work, very little guidance. My manager, as new to the business as I, was happy if I seemed to be getting results. Forget about program structure, forget about sophisticated techniques—does the thing *work?* However, before too many years had gone by, some of the more thoughtful people in the field began to look at what programming really was and the search began for better ways of doing things and, indeed, for getting a handle on just what programmers and programming really are. The search continues.

CRYBABIES AND CLERKS?

One result of the explosion in computer usage over the past two decades is that programmers have always been scarce. Good ones, at least. The field pays well, it promises excitement and fulfilling careers, and lots of people can become programmers. I've worked with many who came from such disparate beginnings as mathematics, chemistry, physics, history, English, teaching, psychological testing, grocery clerking, engineering of all stripes, high school counseling, West Point, the U.S. Navy, and chicken farming. People are given aptitude tests that 80 percent of the population can pass, they're hired and sent to a four-week programming class, and that's it! Now they're programmers. There is still too little intensive training of programmers; the many college-level computer science courses and degrees now being offered are heartening, but they hardly compare to the training routinely given to hordes of electrical engineers.

So what happens? There seems to be a lopsided bell curve representing programming competence: maybe 10 percent excellent, 50 percent competent, 40 percent incompetent. While that's just my wild guess, my reading of books[1] and articles dating from the late seventies leads me to believe that those numbers are not so wild. One author and teacher whose work puts him in touch with many thousands of programmers wonders whether we don't have a lot of clerks holding down programming positions, people for whom programming is just another job and not a profession. In other writings and in conversations over the years, I've often heard programmers called crybabies and whiners. Managers over and over have caved in to programmers' reluctance or refusal to learn a new system or to do the "dirty work" of programming—the documenting, for instance. Managers (including this one) have been guilty of allowing and even promoting an aura of specialness that exempted programmers from doing some of the chores done by any real professional.

FRANKENSTEIN'S PROGRAMMER

Who are the good programmers? What do you want of them? If you were Dr. Frankenstein, how would you assemble one? Along with the bat's blood, you'd want a good brain, a love of logic, a probing inquisitiveness, strong power to concentrate, an amiable disposition, a love of structure, a caring about details and precision, good speaking and writing ability, and a passion for excellence. Add to this list the ability to tie knots and you've got a Boy Scout! These are all qualities you would want in *any* employee, in varying degrees, but you need them all in full measure if you're to have a good programmer. Not everyone in every job needs, for example, to be able to concentrate as fiercely as programmers sometimes must in tracking a piece of program logic through from beginning to end.

I've tried in vain to concoct a formula for a good programmer. I've looked at other people's attempts and found nothing any more helpful than the list of attributes I've just described. What I find myself doing in trying to define good programmers is citing actual people I have known who were *not* good programmers. Some examples:

---

[1]See, for example, Yourdon, as well as Jensen and Tonies.

• James was an excellent technician who could produce more code in a day than almost anyone else around. He loved to let you know that he wrote his code in ink because he rarely needed to make any changes. His worth was limited by his personality, which put people off to the extent that nobody wanted to go to him for help or advice. Most people will not accept advice from anyone who treats them with arrogance. James was incapable of laughing at his own shortcomings, but then, he had none.

• Harry was a cheerful, lovable sort, but his bulb was dim. I'm not being snide. He just wasn't capable of following the intricacies of a program. He knew it and came to feel out of place. He was given a different job, pretty much what we would today call a program librarian. He liked it and did well at it. He was similar to many people in the art field: They like to know about art and work around people who are artists, but they are not creative themselves. The lucky ones know it and don't try to be what they cannot be.

• Larry was lazy except just before appraisal time. He objected to being scored below average or inadequate in any of the appraisal categories, and always wanted more money for what he did. He ranked high in aptitude tests, and he showed signs of intelligence. There were occasional glimpses of neurons at work, but the batteries quickly wore out and Larry relaxed into just making do. A manager can try to inspire a slouch to cast off his sloth, but it's tough to do in a year or so what Mommy and Daddy didn't in twenty.

• Bruce was a slob. He got himself hired during the sixties when companies were trying hard to overlook outward appearances and look for the real person underneath. In Bruce's case, the real person underneath the slob exterior was also a slob. His sloppiness carried over to his work. (You might say, *of course* it did, but that's not always the case. Some very sharp people simply don't pay attention to how they look . . . and smell.) His rats-nest flowcharts were so bad that even the rats would disown them. He did not last long in programming, although a very caring and determined manager did finally get him to improve his appearance and found him work he could do reasonably well.

COMPENSATING THE ACHIEVERS

Wouldn't you like to hire one professional and get rid of ten slugs? In Chapter 1, I discussed the imbalance in compensation for the achievers versus the drones. I bring it up again in this chapter because the problem seems so much more prevalent among programmers than within other disciplines. People in sports who excel command those absurd salaries we all

THE MISSED DEADLINE

Goya, "The Third of May," Museum del Prado, Madrid.

know about. Why not in programming? With a little luck, the drones will find out how much less they're earning than the achievers, and quit.

I'd hate to be thought of as some sort of misanthrope. I don't want anyone to be hurt or not to make a decent wage. I even believe that truly gifted people owe something to the less fortunate. But I don't think the hard workers owe anything to the lazy.

It seems clear that a company can make enormous differences in productivity and quality of output by breaking the usual hiring and compensation habits and, like the U.S. Marines, by looking for a few good people.

PROGRAMMING VERSUS CODING

The programmer is a translator. He or she translates a blueprint into a product, a design specification into a program system.

To varying degrees, almost every programmer does at least some designing, coding, testing, and documenting. The proportion of effort spent in those various facets of the job depends greatly on where he or she works. Some companies look on programmers as coders and attempt to limit the amount of design programmers do—design is for designers. Some companies also limit the amount of testing an individual programmer does, preferring to leave that to a test team. Such severe circumscribing of the programmer's job is self-defeating: Individuals not encouraged to see beyond their little cubicles are not going to add much pizzazz to their company. They'll tend to be clerks putting in their time and not caring much

85

about the company's goals or about a product of excellence. It's imperative that a project be conducted in such a way that programmers are never considered simply as coders. There are practical ways to make this happen.

Stop Design Soon Enough

I talked about this earlier. If you let the designers carry the system design so far that the programs are practically written when the design is finished, you will have missed the chance to establish a strong, meaningful milestone (completion of the design specification) and you will have produced a baseline document too unwieldy, too detailed to be of much use. You will also have robbed the programmers of the chance to be more than coders. That, in turn, means that you limit the chances for a programmer to learn how to design well and move out of programming into other positions, such as analysis and design. Creative people must not be smothered. If your programmers resent being boxed in, they'll eventually go somewhere else where they can breathe. If they don't resent being boxed in, they're probably not worth keeping around.

Move People Around

Analysts often go on to design; some analysts later become system testers; some designers take on the role of lead programmers or programming managers. Assigning people very different jobs on the project during different phases provides needed continuity and gives people a chance to grow (which is to say, it keeps people from being pigeonholed in jobs that are too narrowly defined). As you shift a person from one role to another, however, make sure it's done cleanly, with firm definition of each job. When the design specification is finished and Calvin Designer is about to become Calvin Programmer, take away his designer badge and give him a programming button. Keep your phases clearly defined and separated, and keep people's jobs clearly defined.

It's worth noting here that not everyone *can* be moved around successfully. Some programmers would make rotten analysts, for example, and vice-versa. Don't plug people into places where they obviously don't fit.

DOCUMENTATION

I was either lucky or blind—few programmers who worked for me whined and sniveled about doing documentation. Most of them actually did a decent job of documenting. (My own first manager was not so lucky. My first programs were classic examples of rats' nests, and the documentation proved it.)

However, there are a lot of shirkers out there, and plenty of program systems get delivered for which the program descriptions do not match the program code. That becomes a problem, of course, in program maintenance. The first time a maintenance programmer tries to track down a bug that crawls to the surface after the system is delivered and on the air, he or she stands a good chance of finding programs and documentation that don't match. But even if programs and their listings *do* match, the maintenance programmer is likely to develop a heart murmur simply trying to make sense out of the program's detailed logic.

For both problems—inaccurate documentation and accurate documention of poorly constructed programs—managers have some solutions. The most obvious, but least effective, is to write standards and directives for what you expect in the documentation, and make compliance a requirement for continuing employment. More humane, however, and more sensible in every way is to seek out programming methodologies with built-in documenting enhancements.

Enter *structured programming,* accompanied by a modest blast on the French horns. Structured programming eases the documentation problem in two ways:

- Code is written according to simple rules of indentation intended to lead the reader easily down the page; both the original programmer and the maintenance programmer can follow the code more easily.
- Structured programming restricts the programmer to a small number of powerful coding conventions that nearly eliminate branching from the current page of code to another. In a well-structured program, the reader can follow the code from top to bottom of a page, and from one page to the next, in much the same way as you read this book.

As one of my reviewers pointed out, structured programming by itself won't solve the maintenance documentation problem. Whatever documentation methods are adopted, it's still up to management to *insist* that the guidelines be followed. There's no mechanical substitute for good old management control.

CHICKENEGGCHICKENEGGCHICKEN . . .

The design specification is finished and it's time to turn loose the programmers. How are they to be organized? Did you decide on the programming organization at the beginning of the project? That's the way it's often done. The result is that the finished design is divvied up in a way that fits your organization: Charlie's group gets these pieces, Jill's gets those. In fact, the design process itself might have been affected by the projected programming organization. Let's see, we'll have three programming groups, so we'll start by splitting the design into three major subsystems: the control program, the collection subsystem, the output subsystem. The resultant division of labor might fit the organization chart very nicely, but it might not be the best way to organize the programs. The better approach would be to wait until the overall design is firm, and then organize your programming talent to fit that design.

INTRODUCING NEW IDEAS

Jill Whiz has been managing programmers for about six months. Unsure about managing in the beginning, she feels comfortable now—even enthusiastic about her new job. She calls a meeting of her six programmers.

"Things are going so well that I wanted to let you all know how I appreciate your work. We finished integration test with a few days to spare, and so far, system test has been a breeze."

"Yeah," volunteers Cagney, "and I guarantee those guys in system test won't find much to report. We really wrung the system out before they got it!"

"That's what I think, too," Jill says, smiling. "That's why I've scheduled the whole crew for a three-day seminar starting Monday."

"Great!" cries Lacey. "Where? Is it out of town? Do we get expenses? What's the subject?"

They all laugh at Lacey's priorities. Lacey loves to eat on the company expense account.

"No," Jill answers, "it's right here in Washington, and the subject is structured programming. Ed Certain is conducting it and the timing is perfect for us."

"Why structured programming?" asks Lacey, with a frown.

"Well, Super Software is beginning a push to get everybody trained in the newest techniques—analysts, programmers, the whole bit. Management thinks that structured programming is the place to start."

"Why?" asks Lacey.

"Why what?"

"Why structured programming? What's wrong with what we're doing now?"

Harvey pipes up:"I think our programs are well structured as is. Look how we breezed through integration."

"They are well structured," Jill smiles. "That's why we're good candidates for this class. We already think in terms of good program structuring, so whatever Certain has to offer that's new, we'll be better able to appreciate it and evaluate it than . . . well, than certain other groups in this company. Everybody in this room is a professional, and as professionals we should always be looking for better ways to do our jobs."

"Suppose we listen and decide it's the pits?" asks Lacey.

"Fair enough," replies Jill. "It may be that structured programming has nothing new to offer, but we're the ones elected to find out. If we like what we hear, we get to spread the word to the other groups. If we don't like it, we squash it."

"Why us?" asks Cagney.

"Because we're the best group in the company, and management figures we're the ones to take a look. Peter and Paula and the other project managers agreed we should be the ones to go."

"Sounds good," says Cagney quietly. "I feel good about their choosing us."

A week later, Jill sees Winslow Wimp in the cafeteria and settles at his table. Nobody else is there because people generally avoid Winslow at lunchtime. He's something of a hypochondriac and loves to discuss his current maladies. He's happy to see someone join him.

"Hi, Jill! How y' doin'?"

"Good, Winslow, how about you?"

"Not bad, except for a little bout with labyrinthitis over the weekend."

"Mmmmm! Too bad! Listen . . . " she continues quickly. Damned if she's going to hear a half-hour medical history of his labyrinthitis. " . . . is your group going to volunteer for the next structured programming seminar?"

"Uh-uh! Nope! Waste of time."

"My group really got a lot out of it. They were skeptics going in, but converts coming out."

"What's the big deal? Everybody structures programs. Everybody knows not to write spaghetti-bowl programs anymore."

"But there's more to it than that."

"Like what? Damn! Ear's still buggin' me some!"

"Look, I'd be glad to talk to your group and give them a sort of introduction. Kind of pave the way for a real class."

"No, thanks. Listen, you know what the labyrinth is . . . ?"

People resist change in any number of ways and for lots of reasons, especially lethargy and fear. The ways of selling a new idea are as varied as the number of sellers, but they all boil down to a few:

- *mild threat* ("Your progress in the company depends on your ability to learn and to grow, blah, blah . . . ")
- *serious threat* ("Do it or I'll kill you!")
- *appeal to self-esteem* ("You don't want Jill's people to make us look like monkeys, do you?")
- *opportunity* ("We finally have a break and we can take a few days to look into this new technique.")
- *more opportunity* ("Here's our chance to blaze a new trail for the company!")
- *bribery* ("Do this and I'll remember it when salary reviews come up.")

And so on. You might think that it would be unnecessary to have to sell anyone on improving his or her credentials. It should be, but people do resist. As a manager, you're in a strong position to apply the more humane of the foregoing techniques and finally work your will with your subordinates. But how about convincing *management?* Often the technical people are eager to try new methodologies, but management is slow to go along because:

- If the group spends time going to this class, the project will fall behind. (But there should always be time planned for training.)
- It'll cost too much—there's nothing in the budget. (There should be money budgeted for training.)
- How do we know it'll do any good? (You don't. Some classes will be a waste of time, some ideas deserve to be discarded—but they do deserve a hearing.)
- That's way over the heads of my programmers; better not rock the boat. (Either new programmers or, more likely, new managers are needed.)

Some companies have been bold enough to conduct experiments with new ideas: Separate groups work the same problem using two different methodologies, holding everything except the methodology equal, as far as that is possible. Jill's group can be pitted against Winslow's, both programming the same problem. Such experiments are difficult to conduct because there are so many variables, but the payoff can be great. It takes a fairly enlightened management (or customer) to foot the bill.

THE CORPORATE COCOON

There's a burnout problem among programmers just as there is in any group. You can't expect a programmer to sit for weeks, months, years, doing the same type of programming, and not slack off. If all he or she does is write payroll programs in COBOL, you're eventually going to have on your hands one stale programmer. He or she will pretty soon be doing nothing more than dusting off the last program and applying it to the not-so-new next job—no fresh thinking, no innovation. Who cares? Columnist Hugh Sidey speaks of a "cocoon" in corporate life, where "a group of talented people gather their ideas from the same information base and debate them with one another day after day."[2] Result: stagnation and ignorance of what the rest of the world is doing.

Preventing stagnation is the manager's job. A manager should constantly be training, supporting, coaxing, helping a subordinate to be successful. Don't let your programmers settle for long in cozy nooks, even if they seem to like it. *Get them totally away from their current jobs.* Push them to learn new languages, new methodologies, not only in programming, but in design, analysis, testing, writing. Don't wait until there is a specific job that will require them to retrain. Maybe nobody in your company uses PL/1; maybe they should. Maybe you think ACM conferences and Datamation and language seminars are for eggheads: Do you realize that most modern programming practices are first broached in such forums? Get your people to attend and to read and to question. They can only grow from the experience, and you, your project, and your company can only benefit.

MANAGING PERRY PROGRAMMER

Jill Whiz works for Walt Secondlevel. They are in Walt's office greeting a new employee who has just joined Jill's group.

"Walt," says Jill, "I'd like you to meet Perry."

Walt smiles and shakes hands with Perry and motions Perry and Jill to have a seat. He buzzes his secretary for some coffee.

"So, today's your first day at Super Software!"

"Yes, sir," says Perry quietly, a little nervous.

"Sir!" Walt slaps his thigh and guffaws. "You hear that Jill? 'Bout time somebody around here called me 'sir'!" He enjoys himself while Jill squirms a little and Perry smiles bleakly.

[2]Hugh Sidey, *The Presidency, Time Magazine,* March 4, 1985.

"Let's see, now," continues Walt on a more serious level, "you went to school at . . . Northeastern?"

"Northwestern."

"Right! Well, listen, I want to welcome you to our little company. I hope you enjoy working here. We're pretty new, but growing fast and that means there's a lot of opportunity for anyone who works hard."

"I like what I've seen so far, Mr. . . . Walt . . . I chose this company *because* it's young and growing. I'm anxious to get my first assignment."

"Jill will be taking care of that this morning. Right, Jill?" Jill nods, and Walt continues: "You'll probably find the real world a bit different from what you got at school. . . . " Walt leans back, hands clasped behind his head, and puts his feet on his desk. He spends the next twenty minutes recalling his first job in programming.

A little later, Jill and Perry are finally alone in her office. They sit comfortably facing each other with neither desk nor Walt's feet between them.

"Perry, I know you're anxious to get at your first program, but there are some more important items first." She smiles, sits back and sips her coffee thoughtfully for a moment, then continues: "When I first got into programming, I thought I knew what programming was because, like you, I had taken some courses in college. I found out real fast that I didn't know much of anything about writing a program in an actual business environment. It's a lot more complicated than doing a problem in school . . . but it's a lot more exciting, too!" she adds brightly.

For the next hour, Jill scribbles on her chalkboard and describes to Perry Super Software's business, its organization, how its projects are carried on. She talks about a project life cycle and indicates where Perry's work fits into the cycle.

"It's about time for lunch, so let's go and meet the rest of our group in the cafeteria. After lunch, we'll all come back here and just chat for a while. Then, the rest of the afternoon I'd like to go over some things with you . . . some more introduction to our project. Tomorrow morning, the group will meet here for our biweekly project review. The timing works out well . . . it'll be a good chance for you to hear just what we're doing."

"Sounds super!" says Perry. "After that, will you be giving me an assignment?"

"Sure will!" says Jill.

At the end of the day, Walt Secondlevel saunters into Jill's office as she is clearing her desk to go home. Floyd Hotshot, another first-level manager, is with her.

"Hi, Jill, Floyd! How'd it go with Perry, Jill?" Walt asks cheerfully.

"Fine, Walt. He seems smart and eager. I think he's gonna work out fine."

"Great! What assignment did you give him?"

"The CARDEDIT module," Jill lies.

They chat another minute or so and Walt leaves. Floyd looks at Jill quizzically. "I didn't think you had told Perry yet what his assignment is."

"Right," she says, grinning, "but don't tell Walt that. Listen, when I first came here somebody threw a manual at me, showed me where to sit, and said, 'Here, program a thingamajig.' "

"That's about it," says Floyd, shaking his head in wonderment. "The first time I get somebody new on board I'll sure as hell break him in better. Guess that's what you're up to, huh?"

"Yup! I've even written myself a little checklist." She opens a desk drawer and pulls out a sheet of paper. "This is it. Want to see?"

"Yes . . . " Floyd takes the paper from Jill and quickly skims over it. "Hey, good stuff, Jill! How's chances of borrowing it?"

"Sure. Run a copy and leave the original back on my desk. I've gotta run."

Floyd thanks her and heads for the copier. He decides to stay a few minutes late to look over Jill's checklist. He settles back in his chair and reads.

NEW EMPLOYEE CHECKLIST

FIRST DAY:

1. Meet Walt and Peter Projectmanager.
2. Meet the group.
3. Assign a work space.
4. Describe company and its goals.
5. Describe project organization and how it works.
6. Describe how our group fits in.
7. Discuss generally where employee's work fits in.
8. Give employee copy of company handbook.

SECOND DAY:

1. Have group briefing on project to give technical overview and status. Each member speaks briefly.
2. Assign first task and schedule; group still present.

3. Assign a "buddy" from the group to assist new employee in first assignment.
4. Turn them loose.

ABOUT FIFTH DAY:

1. Meet with new employee and buddy; general assessment of how things are going; work out snags.
2. Meet alone with new employee; general discussion of how things are going; problems at work; if new to area, discuss any moving problems.
3. Now that employee has an idea what we're all about, spend couple of hours going over list of programmer's guidelines.

PROGRAMMER'S GUIDELINES

- The design specs: Stick to them exactly until and unless changed formally.
- Change control procedures: How specs get changed.
- Working with the customer: He's our partner, not the enemy; discuss who's who; will meet customer people soon.
- Coding: No tricky, obscure code; define structured code and set up class if necessary.
- Coding: Detailed design *first*, then code.
- Documenting: How we do it, what tools to use; importance of documentation to a quality product; clean documentation before going on to next module; importance to employee's appraisal.
- Your program module versus the system: Not enough to program brilliantly— it must fit into the system perfectly and must satisfy the specs perfectly.
- Code reviews and structured walkthroughs: What they are; their frequency; your responsibility.

ONE MONTH:

Meet with employee and discuss:

1. Employee's progress.
2. Employee's education. Explain what I can do to help. Discuss seminars, classes, trade magazines, submitting papers.
3. Employee's career. Free-ranging discussion; where does he or she plan to go from here; what's available within the company; what about outside the company? Discuss how promotions and transfers are handled; emphasize that he or she is not limited to advancement only within my group, that I'll always look for good openings even if I have to lose an employee.

Next day, Floyd stops at Jill's office.

"Hey, Jill! Got a minute?"

"Sure, c'mon in."

"Here's your checklist. I made a copy. Listen, I want to tell you, I'm impressed. You go through all that stuff the first few days—the first month—and the new guy's bound to get off to a good start, unless he's a complete nerd!"

Jill is flattered. "Glad you like it, Floyd. I kind of started it when I brought Lacey into the group, and now Perry. Helps a lot. It was easy to write down. I just listed all of the things I wished somebody had done for me when I started . . . "

" . . . and didn't!" Floyd broke in. "I know. Same with me when I joined the company. When I got into this job, though, Bill Goodguy did a pretty good job of getting me up to speed. Still, I don't think even he is this thorough. Mind if I pass this on to him?"

"No, I'd like you to." She bites her lip and adds: "But wait an hour or so. Let me throw a copy at Walt first. Wouldn't want to wound his pride, you know."

Floyd laughs knowingly. "You bet! And thanks . . . See you later!"

Gerome, "Thumbs Down," Phoenix Art Museum, Museum Purchase.

The
Tester

Chapter 5

A newspaper article[1] in 1985 reported the troubles that taxpayers were having with the IRS because IRS had installed a new computer system and was experiencing difficulties with it. Nothing new there. Then the article went on: "As part of the conversion, experts rewrote 1,500 programs—a process that normally requires some debugging."

Well, yes, some.

WHO'S A TESTER?

Everybody: analysts, designers, programmers, managers, customers, and, of course, testers. All through the course of the project, people should be preparing for the next round of testing. Rather than make a product and then figure out how to test it, which is wasteful serial thinking, be planning your tests *in parallel* with the other work. The day integration testing is to begin, know exactly the methodology to be used and have all test cases and procedures and test data ready; the same for system test, acceptance test, and site test.[2] All debate about the conduct of a test should have long preceded that test.

Many more people should be involved in testing than is often the case. It's the worst folly to leave all testing to the programmers. In some ways, they are the least qualified to test their products. That's no reflection on them; even assuming the best of intentions, we can't expect the builder to be the most objective person in the world when it comes to testing his product—he or she will have incredibly dangerous blind spots. Any poor assumptions that went into the building of the product will certainly be carried over to the testing of that product by the builder. Would you want the builder of your house to be the one to pass it through building code inspection? Certainly it's much safer to rely on a licensed inspector (and hope he's not on the builder's payroll!).

There are distinct types of test activity during the project, and managers must make sensible choices of people who participate in each activ-

[1]*USA Today*, Tuesday, March 5, 1985.

[2]For definitions of the various types of testing and ideas about how and when to conduct them, see Metzger, *Managing a Programming Project*. For further excellent coverage of testing, see Ed Yourdon, *Techniques of Program Structure and Design*.

ity. Here are some thoughts about what should be done, by whom, when, and why. *How* is left to other books.

Unit Test

This clearly is the programmer's domain. The individual programmer tests his or her module, with the advice and assistance of co-workers and his or her manager or supervisor. (The manager is—that is, *should* be—involved in all levels of testing, so I won't keep repeating his or her involvement in succeeding paragraphs.)

In "the old days," programmers were left very much alone to conduct unit tests. There was very little guidance and often problems that should have been uncovered during unit tests showed up glaringly during higher-level tests. It's clear to everyone, I'm sure, that the most economical time to find and fix a problem is at the lowest level, where its repair generally involves one module and consumes only one programmer's time. A bug not found until later levels of testing usually involves more people and wastes much more time—and, of course, a bug not found until acceptance test time is a real bummer.

Through the years, there has been more emphasis on controlling unit testing by setting some standards and providing some advice and support, either through a "buddy" system or involvement by the manager or supervisor. A manager can save enormous amounts of later lost time and plenty of all-around grief by getting involved with unit testing. If you manage programmers, set a policy of reviewing (or at least appointing a senior programmer to do so) the unit test plan each programmer has for each module. Unit test plans should not be elaborate, formal documents, like the other test specifications, but simple, handwritten descriptions by the programmer explaining how a specific module is to be tested. You or another programmer can spot a lot and save plenty of wasted test time by looking over such a document. Probably the biggest benefit is that the programmer, knowing somebody is going to go over his or her test plan, will put more thought into it and plan better than if left alone. As a green programmer on SAGE, had someone grilled me about my plans for testing my modules, I'd likely have relied less on single-stepping through hang-up areas.

Integration Test

Execution of integration tests is the job of programmers or teams of programmers during the programming phase. *Planning* for integration testing should be done during the design phase and early programming phase.

In fact, even earlier than the design phase, basic decisions should have been made that directly affect integration: Are you integrating top-down, bottom-up, or some combination of the two? The best of all situations would be to *start* a project with all of your analysis, design, programming, and test methodologies selected.

There's always the tendency to test on the fly. Don't let Sloppy Joe Programmer lull you into bad planning:

"Gee, boss, it's only the design phase of the project. We can't be planning integration tests yet. We don't even know what the programs will look like!"

"But, Sloppy, we do know we're going top-down on this one, and we already have a good pass at the design. So why can't we be looking, for instance, at the set of stubs we'll need at different stages, and the test data we'll need?"

"Well . . . we could, but some of that will change by the time design is finished."

"True, but we'll have a start. In fact, some of our integration planning may have an impact on the design. If you find something awkward or almost impossible to test, sometimes the thing can be redesigned to eliminate the problem."

"Guess so . . . " muses Sloppy.

"What we want, Sloppy, is for integration to be as smooth as we can make it. I'm hoping, for a change, that you guys won't be down at the computer room all hours of the day and night. If we can plan this one right, everybody else in Super Software will take notice."

Sloppy is weakening. That last job *was* a nightmare . . . and he has been wishing he could bring up his salary, but needs a good performance under his belt first.

"Okay, boss, you've got it!" He salutes, clicks his heels, and marches out.

A few days later, Sloppy brings in his rough integration test plan for you to look over.

"Hey, Sloppy," you say, "this is looking pretty good." You resist the temptation to say that this is what you wanted in the first place. "I especially like the way you've outlined how the tests and the test data and procedures are to be packaged. I like nice, neat bundles!"

"Yeah, the more I got into it, the more I liked it. *I'd* like a smooth integration this time myself!"

"Okay, you and the guys go ahead and carry this to the next stage and let me see what you've got, say, at the end of the week. Be sure to keep in close touch with the design crew so that they don't sandbag you by making some radical changes you don't know about."

"Will do. Now, there's something I need to talk to you about. Mind if I close the door?"

Program System Test

Program system testing is performed on the completed program system after the programmers have finished integration test; it is planned and supervised by people other than the programmers. The idea is to test the system against the requirements stated in the problem specification; to test, that is, from the customer's point-of-view. The programmers may have produced an excellent, thoroughly debugged system, but it may in some ways not deliver what the customer wanted. I must confess that, after all these years of advocating this sort of test phase, I'm not sure many actually practice it. Coming as it does near the end of the project, it's easy for it to become a victim of calendar squeezing.

Your system testers should be nasty (maybe a good place for Neander). They must "think customer" and take special delight in making the programmers' lovely product fail. They should be graded on their cunning. They must exercise the system in ways the programmers, narrow-minded fellows that they are, never thought of but in ways that the customer might. The objective is to make the system fail before the acceptance phase, if it's going to fail at all.

As a practical matter, the programmers cannot be kept completely in the dark about what the system testers' plans are. The more information the programming team has, the better for everyone. However, the actual test data that the system testers plan to use should not be available to the programmers, nor should the programmers in any way devise or execute the test procedures. The people doing those chores should not know the programmed innards of the system and should therefore be incapable of manipulating the system in secret and devious ways to get the desired results. The system testers must act the part of the eventual user, who normally will not be someone conversant with programming. A good system test team is your final guarantee (well, almost) that you won't be embarrassed during acceptance demonstration.

The people who are your system testers should be, or at least include, the people who were your analysts. They are in the best position to get inside the customer's head and devise tests to assure that the customer's requirements have been met. However, if your analysts all go on to become designers on this job, they are not suitable as the sole system testers. You need to supplement them with other people who can study the customer's requirements but not know anything of the program system structure. If there is a good salesperson handy, he or she might be very useful in system testing.

Acceptance Test and Site Test

And now for the unveiling. Here, Mr. Customer, is what you ordered!

Acceptance testing, in most cases, ought to be a fairly boring demonstration of the system. The customer should be a key participant in executing the tests and in devising them in the first place. The customer will sometimes insist on introducing data to the system that you haven't seen beforehand; you should not balk at this, but of course you need to be able to determine whether the data are legitimate—that is, do they fall within the bounds specified in your problem specification?

The people you have conducting, or assisting the customer to conduct, acceptance tests are the same people who conducted system tests. Only their demeanor has changed: Rather than a pack of wild animals making life miserable for the programmers, they are charmers, on hand to be of assistance to the customer. No Neanders here, please.

Site tests, if necessary at all, are usually a rerunning of the acceptance tests at each geographical site where the system is to be installed. They generally require the same people as acceptance tests, but some site tests (particularly on military projects) can be extensive and complex and might involve whole new cadres of testers.

When it comes to testing at any level, be a skeptic. No manager can afford to take too much on faith. First-level managers or supervisors must be involved in the test planning. *Know* what's in those test specifications. Question everything. It's not an insult to ask an employee to explain to you how he or she is doing something. Managers in the programming business often are hesitant to interject themselves into the work their people are doing, as though that would somehow indicate lack of trust. It's not lack of trust at all—it's a matter of giving guidance and understanding status, two areas managers are supposed to be good at. Managers must not be afraid to manage.

WHAT GETS TESTED?

Everything. The first thing to remember is that you are testing a system, not simply an isolated program, and the system includes documents and procedures that make the programs usable. The major items include:

Programs

This, of course, is where most of the testing is focused. Programs undergo unit testing, integration, system testing, acceptance demonstrations, maybe site testing, parboiling, wind-tunnel testing, and chemical analysis.

Documents

Unfortunately, this is where there is too little focus. Documents have long been considered evils of doubtful necessity, and they are usually not subjected to any rigorous testing. I'll give you an example that may ring a bell for you. I'm sitting here pecking away at a personal computer keyboard, without which I believe I would never again write a sentence. This thing and its text-processing programs are wonderful (except for a few bizarre happenings now and then)! Yet the manuals that one suffers through in order to get any use out of these marvelous devices try one's patience. If you'll pardon a terrible paraphrase: When a programmer is good, he's very good; but when he writes, he's horrid!

If a programmer's writing is horrid, and if that horrid writing becomes part of a product people pay good money for, then the programmer's management is horrid. Come on now, stop letting that junk get by. I know all the excuses: We ran out of time; the customer cut our funding; tech pubs screwed up; my wife had a baby . . . It's all baloney. The reason for bad writing getting out is the same as the reason for bad programs getting out: Things are not planned well enough in the first place, and not executed well enough in the second place, and not tested well enough in the third place. All that boils down to poor management letting trash get by.

You can do a lot better than the general track record. First, identify the documents that are *really* important. The list might look like this:

- Proposal
- Problem specifications
- Design specifications
- Coding specifications
- User manuals

Concentrate on them. There is plenty more paper around, but most of these are part of the final product and they all usually go to the customer, so sharpen them up first.

Next, schedule the writing, editing, and rewriting of these documents as carefully as you schedule design time, programming time, or test time. Don't treat documents as leftovers. Have them written by people who like to write and are good at it rather than by the programmers who wrote the programs. Talk to the people in the technical publications department, if they are to produce your finished documents. Understand their needs and schedule with them in mind.

Finally, *test* your documents. Some pretty good strides have been made in testing some of them, especially the design and program descriptions, by reviews such as structured walkthroughs. Such critical writings as the user manuals lag behind everything else. That's insane, because they are practically the only tangible items you deliver to a customer to represent your work.

How would you test something like a user manual? Have people who did not write the manual carefully read every word and try to follow the operations described. Enlist the customer's own people very early to help with this chore. Don't simply have programmers try to use these programs; get the user involved.

How about the documents that describe the actual program code? First, never allow a code listing to be delivered that has not been cleanly compiled. At least the delivered documents will agree with the code. That doesn't assure that the *code* is correct in the first place, but that's another subject. Second, you can have the people who are to be the maintenance programmers (often the customer's people) spot-check the code listings for organization, commenting, and general readability.

Procedures

You need to test the procedures necessary for use of the program system. While the testers follow test scripts[3] intended to simulate the eventual customer use of the system, they must pay attention not only to whether something works as specified, but also to whether it was specified intelligently in the first place. Is the system in any way awkward to use? Are instructions or outputs ambiguous? Does the program system do all that it can to reduce manual operations? Are menus clear and concise? Does a given set of actions always produce the same response, or are there differing, confusing responses?

---

[3] See testing in Metzger.

WARRANTIES: A DISTANT GOAL

I dream of a time when programs might carry warranties at least as good as washing machine warranties. Here's how the "warranty" for one of my personal computer programs reads:

THE PROGRAM IS PROVIDED "AS IS" WITHOUT WARRANTY OF ANY KIND, EITHER EXPRESSED OR IMPLIED, INCLUDING, BUT NOT LIMITED TO THE IMPLIED WARRANTIES OF MERCHANTIBILITY AND FITNESS FOR A PARTICULAR PURPOSE. THE ENTIRE RISK AS TO THE QUALITY AND PERFORMANCE OF THE PROGRAM IS WITH YOU.

Is there another product anywhere that gets away with such an incredible cop-out? Maybe it's better, though, than a warranty that promises the moon, but still does not deliver. The U.S. Postal Service, for example, offers overnight express mail and, for a price, guarantees it will get there within twenty-four hours. As I've found out on numerous occasions, it does *not* always get there in twenty-four hours. I've experienced four days' delay. The Postal Service warranty promises your money back, and after much red tape you do get it back, but in the meantime the letter you needed to arrive by some deadline did not make it, and your eleven-dollar or so refund does not make you feel better. So there are honest nonwarranties and there are useless warranties.

We can do better. I may never see a meaningful program warranty, but I do expect to see better programs and better manuals. They will come about when we have better management.

IS THE BUG REALLY GONE?

In the early eighties, I owned an old house that I planned to renovate. Soon after I moved in, I discovered a lot of co-tenants: mice. I bought a "live" trap and set it out every night, and every night I caught a mouse. Each morning I carried the trap back to the edge of some woods about a hundred yards away and let the mouse loose. This went on for weeks. I lost count somewhere, but by the time I had ferried more than thirty mice to their new home in the great outdoors, I began to think that they all looked suspiciously alike. Could it be . . . ? Nah! Yet I still had visions of those mice following me back to the house and sneaking back in (an easy way to get a nightly snack and then to see something of the world in the morning).

I felt pretty silly about this. I didn't think they were smart enough to get back home, but I figured I'd better be sure. I dabbed some paint on the ears of the next few and watched for them to show up again. Well, I caught another ten or so, and then no more. None of them had paint on their ears.

You need to track the bugs during system test the way I tracked the mice. Pay special attention to recordkeeping during system testing.[4] Every time your testers find a problem not caught during integration, it must be logged and tracked until a correction has been made and retesting and regression testing have been completed. Here are some simple rules that, if really honored, will keep you out of trouble during system test:

- When a problem is uncovered by the testers and turned over to the programmers for resolution, it should be logged, given a unique identifier, and assigned to a specific tester for follow-up.
- When a solution is found and tested by the programmers, it should be submitted to the system testers in the form of a newly compiled module or modules with no patches and a fresh listing matching the module.
- The system tester and the programmer should jointly determine how much regression testing is necessary to assure that the repair job to the carburetor did not mess with the ignition. The system tester has the final say, and he or she should be trained to err on the conservative side: When in doubt, retest. Your schedule for system testing must allow for plenty of backing up and retesting (regression testing). The programmer who insists that the fix he made affects only his module should be given a polygraph test.
- Keep a perfectly accurate record of the modules making up any given version of the system being tested. *Never* allow two modules to exist having the same identifier.
- Resist mightily any pressure or temptation to prematurely release versions of your program system to different geographical locations. If the system is not yet through system testing, it ought to remain at the home test site. I have witnessed and been a party to multi-site jobs where the program system sent too early to one site differed from the one sent to another. Suppose you have four sites, and a different version of the program system at each, and testing continues at each site. Can you imagine the mess as different bugs show

[4]See Metzger.

up at different locations, or if even the *same* bugs show up but they get fixed at different times or even in different ways? That situation will quickly get out of control.

Some of your programmers will dislike the logging and tracking business, but the good ones, the experienced ones, will not. Don't put up with the others. Train them, and make them understand the importance of control during testing.

Example:

"But, boss, I did everything we were taught by Certain in that class we took. My module is loose as a goose, hardly any coupling at all. And there are *no* pathological connections, no GOTOs. I tell you, the bug was entirely confined to my module!"

"Hmmmm! My understanding is that in fixing the bug you had to change a flag setting . . . ?"

"Sure, but the only other module that uses the flag is one I wrote!"

"That so?"

"Sure!" A moment's silence. "Except maybe for PRINTX . . . Wonder if it uses it now . . . ?"

Looks like more than one problem here, going all the way back to your basic design. You begin to rethink your opposition to capital punishment.

Example:

Your manager pressured you and you gave in and sent your program system out to four different sites for continued system testing. There were not enough testers to go around, of course, so the programming group was raided and the programmers were pressed into service as system testers. You started everybody off with exactly the same version of the program system and with exactly the same instructions for logging problems.

Now it's two weeks later and you have a mess on your hands. Each day's logs and problem reports are relayed back to your central office by phone, and one of your system testers has the job of coordinating the reports from the four sites. There are now at least four different versions of the system in operation. A bug fixed at one site gets relayed to the others to keep all four systems current, but some get installed slightly differently from one site to the next and some don't get installed at all because the people at the other sites are too busy fixing bugs of their own finding. Sometimes the same bug is encountered simultaneously at all the sites, and it ends up being fixed differently at each site. Sometimes the same bug gets fixed four times at one site in four different ways. You hire a statistician to make some sense out of the pile of reports, but he soon loses contact with reality and has to be locked up. Another couple of weeks and the foul-up is so bad you convince your manager (and the customer who pressured him to pressure you to do this parallel work in the first place in order to save time) that the only thing to do is retreat, start back at the home base with the original "clean" version of the system, and repeat system testing from the beginning.

What I've related has actually happened many times, except for the last part. I don't know of a case where everyone was called home for a restart. You can't afford to lose control of testing. If you don't paint their ears, you'll never be sure those bugs are not returning.

AVOIDING PANIC

The project's managers are gathered around a conference table for the weekly system test report. Floyd Hotshot is standing at the easel pointing to a chart and summing up the week's activities:

"In the B-series of tests, we ran 135 consecutive test cases without an error."

There is a smattering of applause and smiles all around. Peter Projectmanager rubs his hands: "Good going, Floyd!" Floyd continues:

"In the C-series, we successfully cycled the system for fourteen hours before the first problem . . . "

"*Problem! What problem!*" cry all the managers in unison. Two of them pass out and need smelling salts. Sixteen minutes later, the company president has been called in. He announces that the company's forces are to be mobilized and that the National Guard is to be put on standby. He is quite sure that he can get the governor to declare Super Software a disaster area.

Okay, so I'm overdoing it a little bit—but only a little. Our entire upbringing urges us to pounce on problems and make them the center of our activity. Newspapers and TV news shows depend on problems—ever read a whole page or hear a whole half-hour of *good* news? At home and in school bad kids are given lots of attention—the good ones go about quietly doing things well without fanfare. We come under the influence of Tuchman's law: *The fact of being reported multiplies the apparent extent of any deplorable development by five- to tenfold . . . "* In her book, *A Distant Mirror*, she is describing the calamitous fourteenth century, a time filled with chaos, crisis, and bad news, but she could just as well have been describing everyday life on a twentieth-century programming project.

Perfectly rational people do perfectly irrational things when confronted by an apparent project problem. How can you avoid overreacting when problems strike?

1. Put the same emphasis on reporting smooth progress as on reporting failures. That way, a problem is kept in perspective.
2. *Plan* to have problems. Never manage under the assumption that all will go smoothly.
3. Plan to replan. Nobody is smart enough or far-seeing enough to plan any sizable project fully at the outset and never have the plan need any change.
4. Don't be talked into ignoring your good sense and experience. If you reach a point at which a truly tough problem has arisen and it's clear you need more resources, make your stand *now*, get the resources, and proceed with the job. You'll have to take a stand sooner or later—either when the problem first arises and you see the need for help, or later, after you've gone ahead with nothing but hope and have fallen into an even more desperate condition.
5. When you need more resources, don't make foolish tradeoffs. The most common situation is that you need more calendar time, but management and the customer usually will offer you everything *except* calendar time. It has been clearly demonstrated by many experts in the field that adding people or even computer time is rarely the solution to programming problems. Most often, what is needed is more time spent in analysis or design or system test or all three.[5] Time means calendar time, not people-hours. You cannot make up for incomplete analysis or design by throwing more people into programming or testing. What's frustrating about offering this kind of advice is that everybody already knows it. There is only the question of the will and the guts and the integrity to admit what's needed and to act on that knowledge wisely rather than hope that *this* project will be different, and that throwing in eighty-six more programmers will solve the problem.
6. Plan your panic. There may be a time or two on a project when a short period of intense activity is needed to get back on track and make up for a missed milestone. These drills should be rare, and of short duration, if they are to succeed. People who are routinely treated

---

[5] Samuel Johnson, in Boswell's *Life of Johnson* bemoaned " . . . one who looks with unconcern on a man struggling for life in the water, and, when he has reached ground, encumbers him with help . . . "

well will rally and push hard to get things back on track, but they won't do it every other week, nor should they be asked to. Testers, in particular, should be expected to put in some extra hours to do some regression testing and get the project back on schedule. Once that's accomplished, they should return to normal hours. In testing, "normal" is hectic enough.

Daumier, "Rue Transnonain," Courtesy of the Art Institute of Chicago.

The Support Staff

Chapter 6

Once upon a time, the supporters stopped supporting. They all went on strike, and a stillness fell over the office. The phone rang, but nobody was there to answer except managers, programmers, designers, and analysts, and they had long since forgotten how. Typewriters gathered dust and then rusted and fell apart. Programmers' coding sheets piled ever higher alongside the lifeless terminals and finally cascaded to the floor and became stomped into a ruglike mat. The computer winked and blinked at the runs sitting on the table waiting to be executed, but no operator was there to do the loading. File drawers rusted shut from disuse. No one typed anything new to file anyway. Administrative aides were on strike, so no charts got drawn and no progress reports were written, but there was, of course, no progress to report. Three of the brighter managers figured out how to work the coffeepot, there being no secretaries to do so, and finally made coffee, but there was nobody to carry the cups to their desks. Quality assurance people were not around to assure quality, but there were no products being produced, so that was not really a problem.

Finally one day, the head manager, looking wan and resigned, opened the door of his dark office, swept aside some cobwebs, and called to the strikers marching silently in a line around the reception room, carrying signs listing their grievances.

"Okay!" said the head manager. "Okay! I give up! Everybody gets a 20 percent raise!"

The marchers marched and none smiled.

"And an extra week's vacation!"

The marchers marched and none smiled.

"More sick leave!"

The march continued.

In frustration, the manager, tie askew, hollow-eyed, palms out, pleaded: "For God's sake, don't you all know that we *need* you?"

"Ahhhhhh!" chorused the strikers, and they all smiled. The strike was over.

RECOGNITION

Arthur came into my office and settled comfortably in a chair. He looked as though he planned to stay a while.

THE STRIKERS

Daumier, "The Divorcees," Howard P. Vincent Collection.

"Where would this project be without me?" he sighed. I had enough presence of mind not to be flip. The words "probably on schedule" formed somewhere in my brain, but I replied slyly:

"Huh?"

Arthur folded his hands across his belly and continued: "All the programmers who get all of the credit would be pretty bad off if I didn't get their runs to the computer and back on time. Suppose I lost a briefcase over a bridge and into the Potomac?" It was before Watergate, so he couldn't have been involved in that.

"I don't think support people get much notice," he continued. As I leaned forward to give an earnest impression of listening intently, Arthur quickly covered all of the jobs done on the project by people who rarely got any recognition. Although the hour was late and I was tired, I had to agree grudgingly that he had a point, and in a moment of managerial weakness I told him so.

116

"Have any ideas what to do about it, Arthur?" He did indeed.

"A raise would help," he suggested cheerfully. I decided he was so devious that I promoted him to salesman.

Arthur was right. People can accept the less glamorous jobs as long as they are respected for the jobs they *do*, and as long as they are paid in proportion to their worth to the project. It's common for an excellent secretary to be paid less than a mediocre programmer. There are reasons enough: Secretaries are considered easier to replace than programmers; secretaries don't always require a college education, while programmers usually do; administrative people are historically paid less than technical people; secretaries are most often women, and everybody knows women are not worth as much as men. Yet if you consider the worth to the project of Miss Efficient, the secretary, and Wally Whiner, the programmer, there may be no contest at all.

Before we can properly deal with the needs of support people, we need to identify who they are and what their jobs are. On our hypothetical project, I consider a support person to be anyone who is not a manager, analyst, designer, programmer, or tester. Putting it more positively, I would include under support secretaries, typists, keypunchers, librarians, administrative assistants, schedulers, instructors, computer operators, and technical publications people. I'll leave the question of "quality assurance" people for a later section.

You ought to sit down and write a one-page job description for each of your support people—just as you have no doubt done for each of your other employees. If you cannot write anything more meaningful than "responsible for assisting management in reporting progress" or "responsible for secretarial assistance to project manager," either you are operating much too loosely as a manager, or you don't know what your people are doing, or you have people on the payroll who have no real jobs.

Having identified and defined every support job on your project, pay attention to the titles you hang on those jobs. A neighbor named Hilda proudly announced to me one day back in the fifties that she had been given a job at IBM. She said she was to be a sanitation specialist. Her job was to clean toilets. Although IBM sometimes went to goofy extremes, I applaud the idea of defining jobs with an eye to giving them dignity. What's more important than fancy labels for possibly distasteful jobs is to promote the importance of the jobs in the first place. Whom would you rather have out sick for a couple of days: one of your programmers or the fellow who cleans the toilets?

It's easy to take for granted the routine chores that support people handle. Fortunately, it's also easy to turn your head around and look at each job and *see* its importance, and once you've done that, to let the people know that you recognize and appreciate their value. Let them know during routine appraisals of their work and during daily casual conversations with them—those are private times. Also, acknowledge *in public* their importance. What's more bracing than having your boss tell other people how he feels about the value of your work? When awards are being considered, don't just think about manager-of-the-year or programmer extraordinaire; consider typing whiz and librarian-of-the-century. Not many things are accomplished solely by the one who ends up getting the credit. DeeDee Divine may be up for an Academy Award, but where would she have been without her acting coaches, co-stars, supporting actors, her director, her orthodontist, her mommie? When your project finishes successfully and the company throws a shindig for the whole crew, everybody gets invited but the speeches of praise mention the managers by name, maybe, and a few lead technical people by name, maybe, but the support

THE MANAGER WITH HER SUPPORT STAFF

Delacroix, "Liberty Leading the People," Louvre Museum, Paris.

cast is left chewing their creamed chicken and wishing they were up in lights. Recognizing the value of people's service makes them feel good about themselves, about their jobs, and about you. Everybody wins.

BEING OF SERVICE

In the first chapter, I touched briefly on the idea of service: Everyone doing any job ultimately is providing a service for someone else. The work of support people usually is more obviously of a service nature, so it's important that support people feel comfortable with the notion of providing service.

Consider Arthur, who gathers, packages, and transports tapes, disks, and listings between programmers and computer facilities. He is an important link in the chain of events connecting the design of a program with the finished product, a working program. If he delivers late and a run is missed, many programmers may lose a day's compilations or test runs. If he is sloppy about packaging listings, he can cause unnecessary grumbling and loss of efficiency among the many people he is serving. Clearly, he is important to the project—but does he know it? Does anyone make it a point to impress on Arthur the importance of his work?

How about the people who type your correspondence and file your paperwork? Do you realize how important it is to have paper filed in an intelligent way so that it can be retrieved without wasting valuable time? Is it important to you to have your letters, memos, and reports done expertly, with style and accuracy? Your written work says a lot about you to the people who read it. I remember a simple comment made by a fellow named Russ one day to my secretary, who had typed a letter for him: "Shirley, you sure type a nice letter! Thanks!" Shirley blushed with pleasure and I took note: When was the last time *I* had complimented her on her work?

While emphasizing the idea of being of service, it's necessary to raise one red flag: Support people should do everything possible (within moral and ethical bounds) to further the objectives of those they support, but they should not be expected to do hatchetwork. A manager faced with a distasteful task (such as firing somebody) should not have a staff assistant carry the bad news. I realize this is done all the time, especially in politics, but I think a decent and caring manager owes it to those who work for him or her to deal with them directly on important and personal matters. It's not only humane; having to face up to onerous chores makes one think harder about the rightness of the act.

NO DUMPING ALLOWED

Support areas often are a dumping ground, or at least a holding area, for people nobody knows what to do with. There are several categories of people-nobody-knows-what-to-do-with: Manny Manager did not quite hack it on his last assignment and nobody wants to take a chance having him manage again; Sally Seller is bright as a star, but lacks the personality to get along with "those dumb customers"; Eugene Engineer, whose training was in the field during the good old days of card punches and abacuses, has seen technology pass him by; Primitive Programmer still doesn't trust high-level languages and operating systems.

The list is long. Yet looked at in another way, the list of dumped people probably boils down to two categories: (1) those who are incompetent, lazy, obnoxious, disruptive, and refuse to do anything except what they are accustomed to doing, and (2) those who may be in the wrong niche, but who obviously are of value to the company. I've seen very few in category 1. They generally deserve to be fired; a company's responsibility toward salvage operations has a limit somewhere. Most are in category 2, and organizations generally have two ways of dealing with them: retrain them or dump them.

Retraining, whether done through formal classes or on the job, is nearly always a profitable venture for the company. It's the smart and loving thing to do. You end up with someone newly trained in *B* who also has experience in *A*, and that's a plus. Not only is the retrained person more versatile, but he or she is likely to be more loyal, as well, which translates to a happier person and better productivity.

Dumping means assigning someone to a project and trying to keep him or her busy. If the project needs help and this person can fill a real need, fine. However, the project often has neither the need nor the budget for another body, and the dumpee hangs around trying to be either useful or invisible. The dumpee is assigned to a manager who has enough to do already and now must work at finding something for the dumpee to do.

Many people are stuck into slots that are strictly make-work; they often are assigned to "quality assurance" groups or made "administrative assistants." Frequently, the dumpee's assignment is called on-the-job training, but it's only another term for nothing to do.

I have vivid recollections of dumpees. Some crept into dark corners and tried not to be noticed. Some found meaningful work to do and became useful. Some found unnecessary work to do and made life miserable for other project members by involving their time in this unnecessary work. And many wandered the halls grumbling and complaining and being generally disruptive. They became the well-known rotten apples in the barrel.

An un-busy person among many busy people can cost you a whole lot more than just his or her wasted salary; he or she wastes a terrific amount of other people's time.

In the company division where I worked, it was fairly common for people to be without meaningful work for periods of weeks or even months. I remember a particular time when a group of four or five dumpees spent an entire day compiling a list of clichés, for no particular reason. I still have it. It's four hundred entries long, and cost the company about a thousand dollars.

In this same division, there was a whole group of dumpees who were told to write some sort of quality assurance regulations. They measured their success the way proposal writers do: by the volume of paper they produced. The bigger the pile got, the more certain that no one would ever use it. And as they wrote their rules and drew their charts and checkoff lists, they wasted the time of people other than themselves, people such as I who had to read and comment on their work.

However, the dumpees who are actually harmful are those who spend their time complaining about management, the company, and the world in general. Those people cost the company a great deal in terms of the lost productivity of the people whose ears they fill daily with their grumblings. Un-busy people often are the worst troublemakers and morale-killers.

Again, what's the alternative to having spare people assigned to your programming project? Train them for other jobs, but keep them in a training pool until legitimate jobs are available. *Don't* assign them to specific projects where they are really not needed. If they are going to consume company funds while being retrained and awaiting assignments, have them do so in a group or department set up specifically to handle them, rather than siphon off the energies of projects that have no current need for more bodies.

QUALITY OF LIFE

The veal on the dinner table last week came from an animal whose entire life was spent in a tiny enclosure, practically unable to move, fed on a diet deliberately deficient in iron so that its meat would be pale and tender. Not much quality of life there. Lots of secretaries, typists, librarians, and other support people spend the working part of their days the same way. They occupy mental cubbyholes where they do their work almost mechanically. They could do the same work, but *better,* and with more *enjoyment*—all that's missing is some nourishment, some understanding of how their work relates to the overall project.

DUMPEES AT WORK

Daumier, "Three Gossiping Women," Courtesy Wildenstein Gallery, New York.

Consider a typist who sits all day typing memos or technical documents with little notion of what the documents mean. One theory is that a good typist can type anything perfectly without understanding content, but think how mind-dulling that has to be! Wouldn't anyone have more fun typing a draft of *The Joy of Sex* than a treatise on laser beam theory? If your reaction is "Since when should a job be fun?" I fear you may have been born into the wrong era and might be more comfortable managing a nineteenth-century sweatshop. I have tried to make the point in as many ways as possible in this book that a good manager will consciously seek out ways to make more enjoyable the working lives of those for whom he or she is responsible.

If your typist has even a rudimentary understanding of programming, typing the programmers' technical jargon will be easier and the results more accurate. Consider this conversation between Tessie Typist and Pancho Programmer:

"Tessie, I'm afraid this draft will have to be redone."

"Oh, no! What's wrong, Pancho?"

"Well, first of all, you've changed the indentation here where I've written these program instructions."

"Well, gee, when I type a memo I use the rules of indentation I've been taught. What you wrote looked like a mess!"

"Ummmm, well, you see, when you write program language instructions, the indenting is meaningful. It's not the same as with ordinary text."

"Sorry, Pancho, I didn't realize . . . "

"And another thing, you changed some lowercase to uppercase, and vice versa—they all need to be typed just as I wrote them."

"Mmmmm! I'm real sorry, Pancho. I'm so used to typing nontechnical stuff on my last job. Well, let me fix this . . . "

Fortunately, Tessie types using a word processor, so the fixing is not a big deal. Were she working with a plain typewriter, the story would be different. Still, time has been lost and feelings bruised. Had Tessie been given a short course in "programming for nonprogrammers," both the lost time and the bruises could have been avoided. Even a rudimentary understanding by all project members of what the project is about will pay off every single day. Training Tessie in programming is *not* a waste of time.

Training your nontechnical people in technical subjects is not expensive. You don't expect Tessie to write programs, only to have a feel for the jargon, so her training need not get into actually coding anything. You can get her off to a good start with the expenditure of only two hours a day for a week or so; the time can be spread out to fit her workload. Topics covered might include an understanding of computers, programs, and

SURE, I'D LOVE TO TYPE IT OVER

Villon, "Renée du Trois-quarts," The Baltimore Museum of Art, Museum Purchase.

programming languages, with some very simple examples of programs coded in the project's languages and a description of how they work.

The same basic training would be appropriate for other support people. The training can be carried further for those whose support work involves more interaction with the programmers than typing their technical materials and correspondence. Librarians and computer operators, for example, would benefit from much more extensive training than that given typists.

CREDIBLE SUPPORT

I was sitting across the desk from Danny, a programming manager on a large defense project. The mail boy breezed in, deposited a thick envelope, and left. Danny put aside his coffee cup, peeked inside the envelope, and proceeded to comment heatedly on the ancestry of someone named Barney.

"What's the fuss?" I asked.

"Barney! He's cranking out paper again!" Danny spread out the contents of the envelope. The impressive-looking page headings read something like this:

- Project 599L
- Office of Standards and Procedures
- Date
- Standard: STD-100-A/6
- Application: All Programming Managers
- New Pages: xxx.1 and xxx.2
- Replacement Pages: aaa.4 - aaa.9
- Deletion Pages: aaa.10,11
- Summary of Standard: . . .

Attached were the new pages to be inserted into the Standards and Procedures Manual. Danny leaned back and snatched his copy of the S and P manual from his bookshelf. There were two volumes, each in a two-inch thick binder.

"Dammit!" he spat. "The standards are thicker than the program listings!" He swore a little more and then, feeling somewhat cleansed, leaned back with his hands clasped behind his head.

"What do they get for scrap paper these days?" he wondered.

"About a nickel a hundred pounds."

"Let's see . . . at that rate, we could sell all these manuals and get the project back in the black!"

We traded wry comments about the standards manual for a while until we tired of the sport. Then Danny, now sober, got to the nub of things:

"There are two things wrong with this manual," he began.

"I know," I broke in. "Volume one and volume two!"

"No," he said, grinning. "Volume and Barney."

"I don't follow."

"Well, the sheer volume is way out of line. There's so much in here that nobody bothers using any of it. It's full of needless crap. It tries to tell you how to do everything but tie your shoes!"

"Page ninety-three, paragraph fourteen!"

Undeterred, Danny continued: "But the other thing that's wrong is Barney. Barney is a *very* nice guy, but the people around here won't listen to him."

"Why not?"

"No credibility. He has no technical background, so every time he puts out a standard, it's suspect—no matter who originated it. You've got to have a guy in that job who has enough technical experience that the people on the project respect his judgment and listen to what he puts out."

"But he doesn't just pick these things out of the air. Management signs off on them all."

"Not good enough! Managers get too busy and rubber-stamp things they shouldn't. No, you've got to start with somebody who knows programming to begin with. That guy will get listened to."

"Okay!" I laughed, "I'm convinced!"

"Good!" Danny grinned. "I've recommended you for the job!"

"I'll kill you!" I said, and left his office.

Two days later, I had a new assignment.

THE RIGHT TOOLS

There's no reason your support people should labor with old tools while your programmers are playing with the latest computers, languages, compilers, and test and documentation aids. In particular, your secretaries, typists, and program librarians ought to be using "smart" typewriters and small computers to handle typing, storing, and retrieving all kinds of data. As many of you know, there is no going back to your old, manual Remington after using, say, an IBM Selectric; in the same way, ordinary electric typewriters are pure drudgery once you have whipped out a piece of writing using a word processor. Even the smallest computer with word-processing capability allows one to type, edit, and print a page much faster and much more accurately than any regular typewriter—and it allows you quick and easy filing and later retrieval as well.

The cost of small processors and smart typewriters is no longer prohibitive. For the cost of a couple of electric typewriters, you can buy a small but powerful word processor and throw out your correction fluid, erasers, and carbon paper. There is scarcely anyone on the project whose tasks cannot be performed better with the aid of a desktop computer. For example:

- Secretaries and typists can originate, edit, and duplicate documents quickly and easily.
- Librarians can file and catalog documents and retrieve them on demand; lists of available documents can be sorted and updated and produced at will.
- Managers and administrative aides can bring together project status data from multiple sources and combine them to produce status reports without the need for cutting and pasting documents. All kinds of charts can be maintained, modified, and printed without the laborious business of drawing and redrawing charts.
- Computer time schedulers can keep track of available time and how the time is to be distributed among the users.

The biggest hurdle, when converting from typewriter to word processor, is retraining. Some people firmly attached to the good, old methods will balk—but once a typist has tapped out a memo, clean and without error, without having to erase or start over on a clean sheet of paper, he or she will be converted for life.

QUALITY ASSURANCE

Cal Quality brings the meeting to order by rapping his brass knuckles on the table.

"Okay, you guys," he begins, in a vain attempt at a Jimmy Cagney impersonation, "you dirty rats, let's see what quality work you're putting out."

The programming managers try desperately not to make eye contact with one another. The slightest smirk and they'll all break up before the meeting even gets underway. They tolerate goofy Cal and try to keep these meetings as painless as possible.

"Jerry," says Cal, "let's look at your programs first. Now, my list says you've completed and turned over to the library CPCI's numbered twelve through seventeen."

"Ummmm, yeah, Cal, except that their real ID's are different."

"Jerry, couldn't you number your programs the way we do so we don't get all confused? The Air Force insists that we use CPCI nomenclature."

Jerry mutters something obscene and then says aloud: "Cal, halfway through the project you come along and want us to throw out our entire way of doing things just to conform to an idiotic configuration management scheme originally meant for hardware, not programs. The system is unnatural and uncomfortable. It's force-fitting software into molds made for hardware!"

"Jerry, what's the difference what you *call* something? The product is still the same."

"Exactly! So let's use our standard names and forget this CPCI bull!"

"Can't, Jerry. Customer insists."

Jerry sighs. The meeting drones on. Cal calls out identifications of deliverable items, and Jerry and the other programming managers point to appropriate piles of listings and disks carefully stacked on a table and testifies that such and such disk and listing are indeed the item that Cal has called out from his checklist. So help them, God.

When the meeting is over, there is agreement that the stack of programs on the table agrees with Cal's list of items promised to the Air Force at this stage of the project.

So lists are made to agree, cosmetics are attended to; but deep in the stack of disks is one that replaced its original just before the meeting to correct a very minor, late-found bug. The printed listing does not agree with the changed disk. Further down in the pile are several listings whose identifiers have been altered because someone had found several pairs of programs with the same identification symbols. There is some question whether the appropriate ones were corrected.

This is a project in trouble. There is a loss of change control, among other things, but compounding the other problems is the imposition of a separate "quality assurance" function with good intentions but fighting a losing battle.

I have always felt that quality assurance is the job of the managers responsible for the product. A separate group can't "assure" much if the responsible managers have not done their jobs properly. A separate group is a layer of bureaucracy that can cost a lot and not necessarily produce much. Managers should be held responsible for quality and not allowed

THE QUALITY ASSURANCE BOARD

Daumier, "The Legislative Belly," Courtesy of the Art Institute of Chicago.

to slough off part of their responsibility to a group whose name sounds right but which cannot be expected to guarantee quality if the responsible managers have not been able to do so.

If your project is organized to include a separate quality assurance group, whether you like it or not, there are some sensible things you can do to make the scheme work better:

1. Make sure the quality assurance function is planned for at the beginning of the project, not after you are already well along. Settle early all matters of responsibility, procedures, and nomenclature.
2. Don't make the quality assurance group a dumping ground for people not otherwise gainfully employed. Look for people not only knowledgeable in the quality assurance procedures your customer requires, but in the programming business. Don't assume that a hardware quality assurance person can automatically do a competent job in software.
3. Don't let quality assurance become a sort of pseudo-management. Have quality assurance people support management, not replace it.

MANAGING SUPPORT PEOPLE

There is no trick to managing support people. Just remember that they *are* people and need the same caring and understanding as the programmers. Don't be absurd and tell every person he or she is so critical to the project that the project would die without him or her. Don't use puffery. Just honestly let each person know he or she counts.

The way a manager interacts with people he or she is responsible for is a personal matter, but here are some guidelines you might find helpful:

1. Practically every secretary is a typist, but not every typist is a secretary. Respect the secretary's status and make the position one to which a typist might aspire. Don't make the title "secretary" meaningless by giving him or her nothing but typing and filing jobs; make the job more responsible. Your secretary can help you to manage your time, usually a manager's scarcest commodity. A good secretary can organize your files in an intelligent, orderly way—something my first secretary tackled immediately. It's usually a good idea to make clear which secretary or typist handles whose work—for instance, perhaps secretaries handle the managers' typing and typists handle everyone else's. Try for enough harmony and flexibility that when one person is overloaded, it's natural for the other to come to the rescue. That's not so easy if you allow a situation to arise where there's too much concern about turf. For example, a secretary who looks down on doing a task normally assigned to a typist is someone who has been allowed more insulation than is good for your project.

2. Encourage support people to help define their own jobs and to offer ways of doing those jobs better. Arthur, who shuttles between programmers and computers, can and usually will develop refinements to the procedures for submitting and retrieving computer runs if he knows his suggestions will get a thoughtful response (something other than, "Oh, that's just Arthur's idea—what does he know?"). Keep your ears and mind open to what these people have to say. Their working lives *are* the support services they offer; if they are good workers, they are bound to come up with better ways of fitting their jobs to the needs of the project.

3. Make up your mind that support people will not replace management. There are at least two areas in which I've seen this happen. The first is when administrative assistants are given so much apparent authority that the feeling gradually forms that they always speak for management and that they are, in fact, tantamount to management. The second instance is that of quality assurance people or

sometimes system test people whose role becomes so strong that programmers and others begin taking direction from them to the exclusion of management. There are other examples: strong-willed secretaries replacing namby-pamby bosses; salary administrators playing God by jerking purse strings; computer operators deciding they know better than management how to assign computer time priorities. This may sound as though I think managers should have godly status, never to be challenged, but that's not my point. Managers exist to plan, direct and control the project. Part of the way they control is to listen to and weigh advice. Once a decision is made, that's the way things should proceed until a new decision is reached. Erosion of management decisions by people who always "know better" undermines managers' credibility and can bring a project to grief.

Munch, "The Cry," Museum of Fine Arts, Boston. William Francis Warren Fund.

The Customer

"Do you, Super Software, Inc., take this fellow to be your lawfully contracted customer, till death do you part?"

"Well, I don't know about this death bit . . . "

"How about 'till product is delivered'?"

"Yeah, okay, I'll buy that. Right! I mean, I do!"

"And do you, Mr. Customer, take Super Software, Inc., to be your lawfully contracted contractor?"

"Well . . . "

"Come on now, I've got other things to do! Yes or no?"

"Well, okay, I guess, but I've got to like the product!"

"That okay with you, Super Software, Inc.?"

"I think so, but what if he doesn't like anything I do?"

"Yes or no?"

"Ummmm, well, I guess, sure, but . . . "

"By God, make a decision!"

"Yes! Okay! I will! I mean, I do!"

"About time! I now pronounce you contractor and customer. You may embrace."

"Now, wait a minute!"

THE HONEYMOON

The courtship has ended. It's time to build a lasting relationship with the customer. Depending on how new the customer people are to you—you may have flirted with them on a prior contract or certainly during the proposal stage—you may have to spend considerable time getting to know them. You'll need to find out who is responsible for what, who speaks with authority, who is likely to be a weak link, who plays politics, whom you can rely on for accurate data. Meanwhile, of course, the customer is learning the same things about you.

Project managers often enter into a contract in a negative frame of mind—there is a sort of adversary relationship, rather than a partnership. That's totally crazy, since both of you want the same thing: a smooth project and an excellent product. Managers need to be careful how they speak about the customer. Wry comments or nasty customer jokes are likely to be picked up by your project people and translated into a general negative view of the customer. If you go about referring to one of the customer's people as a fool, that's how your subordinates are going to view him. Don't forget, like it or not, managers are role models and their behavior will be mimicked by others in subtle (and often anything but subtle) ways.

Your dealings with your customer must be honest. You do not have

BLISSFUL MARRIAGE

Wood, "American Gothic," Courtesy of the Art Institute of Chicago.

to love your customer, although that would be wonderful, but you must be honest with each other. One difficult job I worked on was made more difficult because our management and the customer's management both came to understand early that the contract job definition was seriously flawed, politics having played a strong hand, yet neither could admit this publicly. It was a strain that was to affect the entire job negatively. Neither side had the courage or the will to admit errors, set them right, and proceed from there. If your management finds itself spending lots of time in meetings discussing strategems for sidestepping the customer, take that as a warning that the project is in trouble and that you need to refocus on your relationship with the customer. I am not talking about ordinary disagreements that arise between any two groups of people. I am referring to deeper problems that keep you awake at night.

Some contracts work smoothly *because* of personal relationships that click. I managed a number of small jobs that were very successful because the individuals involved—a programmer named Jim on one job, for example—were honest, personable, and technically competent. (I was made

136

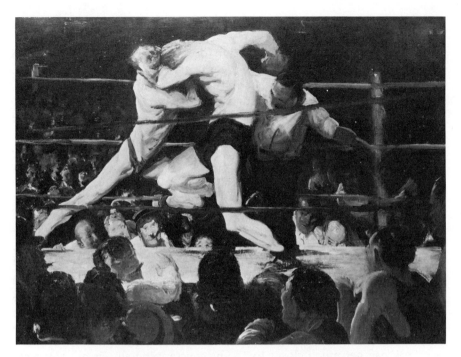

WORKING THINGS OUT WITH THE CUSTOMER

Bellows, "Stag at Sharkey's," The Cleveland Museum of Art, Hinman B. Hurlbut Collection.

to look good on plenty of jobs because of the excellence of the people I was fortunate enough to have working for me.) The only problem with projects that work well because of personal relationships is that nobody is permanent. Jim's replacement might not hack it at all with the customer that Jim got along with so well.

FIDELITY

Well, where do things stand this week, Mr. Contractor? Oh? But I thought those modules were reported done last week? Ah, I see. Somebody found one more little bug. Well, those things happen . . . guess you'll have to revise your bar charts, eh? I mean, since you showed this module 100 percent done last week. What's that you say? Now they're 110 percent? Ha! Ha! That's a good one, by golly! What? You're serious? Listen, what is this—a football game? Jocks always give 110 percent, but programs . . . ? You know, I'm beginning to worry about you.

Unfaithfulness in reporting can begin small and pretty soon the marriage is ruined. Once the customer begins to lose his trust in you, it is very difficult to rebuild. Obviously, you must try to prevent erosion in the first place.

Inaccurate reporting occurs in two forms: (a) through dishonesty, and (b) through confusion in your own organization about where things stand. Although dishonesty gets the headlines, I don't think it is the more common scenario. Periodically, whistle-blowers in government and industry make a lot of noise by exposing skulduggery, and it happens on smaller projects the public never even hears about. I'm not addressing such felonies here. I'm interested only in form (b). Everyone knows that understanding the exact status of programming jobs is tough. For example, other writers have demonstrated the near-impossibility of testing every path in even a fairly simple program. But this section is not about testing—it's about reporting status as clearly and honestly as you can.

The single, most important requirement for accurate reporting of status is defining a realistic and sensible base against which to measure. Everyone knows that it's a foolish exercise to describe the completion of program modules in terms of "percent complete." There is no telling when you are 50 percent done, since tonight's computer run may expose a bug that will set the progress clock way back. Yet it's not enough to say "It's done when it's done." You and the customer need better information than that.

You can get much closer to Truth by scrapping all percent complete reporting. A better scheme is to report only on the status of two kinds of items: (1) *tangibles,* such as technical reports, analysis documents, design documents, test plans, user manuals, and even "completed" code; and (2) specific *events,* such as the execution of test cases. A list of the reporting items for a program module, for example, might be:

- Detailed module design complete
- Module coded
- Module compiled; no compilation errors
- Test case #1 executed successfully
- Test case #2 executed successfully
- Test case #3 executed successfully
- Test case #4 . . .
- Test case #n . . .
- Module documentation corrected and clean compilation
- Module submitted for integration

There are some "ifs" and "buts" even about this approach. If, say, test case #3 fails and a program change is made, then test case #3 is not reported successfully executed until appropriate regression testing (probably rerunning #1 and #2) has been done. Likewise, clean compilations must be obtained and regression tested when program changes are made. What is important is that you have the most stable items possible to report on and that the items must be meaningful. It would be self-defeating, for example, if test cases 1 to n-1 were trivial and test case n were a crusher. The approach is not foolproof and you can still get into trouble if you do not construct your list of items thoughtfully, but this method is a great deal more accurate and meaningful than the thoroughly discredited percent complete scheme.

As important as constructing a reporting scheme that makes sense is the explanation of that scheme. Describe to the customer just what your list of items means and what a report of "complete" for any item means. Describe how regression testing can influence the report from one week to the next. Point out the degree of inaccuracy inherent in the system. Having done all that in your most honest and earnest way, you can now expect the customer to be, week by week, no more confused than you.

CHANGE

In *Managing a Programming Project*, I have a lot to say about changes in the work scope during a project and offer a simple mechanism for controlling change. Here I want to emphasize that whatever change control procedures you employ, they will work better if you educate your customer. If the customer knows exactly how a change request should be made and how you intend to handle each request, strife over proposed changes will be minimized.

It's important to realize that there can be no meaningful discussion of a change if you and the customer cannot even agree that what is being proposed *is* a change. He or she may feel that what is being proposed fits within the original work scope. There is only one way to avoid that problem: the job must be accurately defined in the contract or at least in the problem specification written early in the project by your analysts.

STEPCHILDREN

You may have to live with some of the customer's programmers or other customer people joining your own to work together on the project. Make sure you have control over them if your success is partly dependent on their work, and be wary of assigning them tasks on your critical path.

There is another aspect of this that can get touchy. The "borrowed" customer people—usually programmers—might like what they see in your company and want to leave home and join you. You must avoid even the

ONE MORE LITTLE CHANGE, BOYS!

David, "Death of Socrates," The Metropolitan Museum of Art, Wolfe Fund, 1931.

appearance of pirating. When customer employees make overtures, the only reasonable thing to do is tell them straightforwardly that, under the circumstances, you cannot even consider hiring them until the contract has ended or unless they first openly inform their management that they want to apply to you for employment. Even so, you may not be interested in hiring them, and if that is the case you need to persuade them, gently but firmly, that until the project ends there can be no consideration of hiring. There are all kinds of possibilities here; the best advice is to be sensitive to what's happening and avoid encouraging anyone to jump ship.

OTHER OFFSPRING

Jake Customer answers his phone: "Hello! Jake here!"

"Hello, Jake! This is Pete Projectmanager. How are you?"

"Fine, Pete. What's up?"

"Well, now that we're underway on the project—and doing nicely, I might add—I'd like to touch base with you about how we might work together in the future."

"Oh? What future work do you have in mind?" Jake's fingers begin tapping his desk-top.

"I hear you're thinking about automating your gum machines."

Jake sits upright. "Where did you hear that?"

"It's pretty common knowledge."

"Well, that's something! I'm gonna have to plug these leaks somehow!"

"I won't spread the word, Jake. Trust me." Jake shudders. He trusts no one. "But anyway, do you think we might have some informal talks about it. By the time you're ready to roll, we might have some decent ideas to offer."

Jake pauses. "Peter," he begins slowly, "it's a little early. We're barely into the current project. And by the way, I understand we missed the first milestone."

"The problem spec . . . Yes, it's a little late, but . . . "

"When we do the gum machines, I want to be sure we go with the right contractor. It'll be a sticky job."

"Sure, sure, Jake. Well, listen, we'll talk more. Just wanted you to know Super Software is ready to serve you!" He manages a hearty, but hollow, laugh and ends the conversation.

Conceiving follow-on work only makes sense if the marriage is going smoothly. Don't talk about follow-on jobs before showing that you can handle the current one. You may wonder why I take up space stating the obvious: I've experienced first-hand the dilution of effort on a new contract by expending effort too soon on follow-on. In each such case I have witnessed, the result was negative. One customer, an important one, finally put his foot down and told the project manager: "Don't talk to me about *xyz*; let's see if you can do *abc* first!"

HAPPILY EVER AFTER

Break your vows and expect divorce. Be caring, honest, and hard-working, and look for a happy relationship.

If you treat your customer as a nuisance or a "necessary evil," you're in for trouble. Think of the people you've dealt with in life when *you* were the customer. There are incredible numbers of people out there who have no business facing a customer—people who are surly, unsmiling, or just don't give a damn. Those who make you feel welcome stand out because they are so rare. They are the people you are most likely to go back to.

Returning to the idea of *service*, if you can be happy providing excellent service, you have a shot at a successful relationship with your customer. If you give service grudgingly, you have an unhappy time ahead of you.

Miller, "Jude," Courtesy of the artist.

Make
A Difference

Chapter 8

In July 1985, I was one of some sixty people who staged an illegal sit-in and takeover of offices at the National Institutes of Health in Bethesda, Maryland, just outside Washington. Our goal was to shut down the University of Pennsylvania's Head-Injury Clinic. This was a place where, thanks to tax-supported funding by NIH, various primates over a period of many years had been subjected to the most brutal treatment imaginable. The clinic sought to discover the effects of traumatic injury to the head such as might be sustained in a football game or an automobile accident. The method was to use various ingenious devices to inflict damage on the skulls of helpless captive primates. A baboon, for example, would be confined in a harness and have its head rammed by a jackhammer-like contrivance. Then it would be examined to determine what effect the blows had had.

The story is long and involved. The happy ending is that the four-day civil demonstration succeeded in a dramatic way. Health and Human Services Director Margaret Heckler, President Reagan's cabinet official who had jurisdiction over NIH, agreed over the vehement objections of NIH officials to suspend funding to the head-injury clinic, pending an investigation. Shortly after, funding was cut off completely and the clinic was out of business. Hundreds of defenseless animals from among the millions mutilated and savaged each year in laboratories around the world were saved from lives of extreme pain and helplessness.

I am not a born activist. I get nervous when a waiter looks at me with disdain. I'd like it if everyone would just "be nice." Yet much later in my life than I like to admit, I've begun to learn about standing up for things that matter. I've learned that I can make a difference.

As a manager, every single move you make will influence dozens, hundreds, perhaps thousands of people. That's not a thought for the faint-hearted. Your influence can be positive or negative, major or minor. If you go about your job in a caring way, with genuine concern for the people around you, your business goals will be successfully reached or exceeded, and everyone will enjoy the trip.

You *can* make a difference.

References

ARON, J. D., *The Program Development Process* (Reading, Mass.: Addison-Wesley, 1983).

AUGUSTINE, NORMAN R., *Augustine's Laws* (New York: Viking Penguin, Inc., 1983, 1986).

BIGGS, CHARLES L., EVAN G. BIRKS, and WILLIAM ATKINS, *Managing the Systems Development Process* (Englewood Cliffs, NJ: Prentice-Hall, Inc., 1980).

BOEHM, BARRY W., *Software Engineering Economics* (Englewood Cliffs, NJ: Prentice-Hall, Inc., 1981).

DEBONO, EDWARD, *The Five-Day Course in Thinking* (New York: Basic Books, 1967).

DEMARCO, TOM, *Controlling Software Projects* (Englewood Cliffs, NJ: Prentice-Hall, Inc., Yourdon Press, 1982).

GLASS, ROBERT L., *Modern Programming Practices* (Englewood Cliffs, NJ: Prentice-Hall, Inc., 1982).

——, *Software Reliability Guidebook* (Englewood Cliffs, NJ: Prentice-Hall, Inc., 1979), Chapter 1.

JENSEN, RANDALL W., and CHARLES C. TONIES, *Software Engineering* (Englewood Cliffs, NJ: Prentice-Hall, Inc., 1979).

KEPNER and TREGOE, *The Rational Manager* (New York: McGraw-Hill, 1965).

MALTZ, MAXWELL, *Psycho-Cybernetics* (New York, NY: Pocket Books, 1969), pp. 19–20.

METZGER, P. W., *Managing a Programming Project* (Englewood Cliffs, NJ: Prentice-Hall, Inc., 1981).

PAGE-JONES, MEILIR, *Practical Guide to Structured Systems Design* (Englewood Cliffs, NJ: Prentice-Hall, Inc., Yourdon Press, 1980).

PETERS, L. J., *Software Design: Methods and Techniques* (Englewood Cliffs, NJ: Prentice-Hall, Inc., Yourdon Press, 1981).

STRUNK, WILLIAM JR. and E. B. WHITE, *The Elements of Style* (New York, MacMillan Publishing Co., 1979).

YOURDON, EDWARD, *Techniques of Program Structure and Design* (Englewood Cliffs, NJ: Prentice-Hall, Inc., 1975).

YOURDON, EDWARD, and LARRY L. CONSTANTINE, *Structured Design: Fundamentals of a Discipline of Computer Program and Systems Design* (Englewood Cliffs, NJ: Prentice-Hall, Inc., 1978).

YOURDON, EDWARD, *Managing the Structured Techniques* (Englewood Cliffs, NJ: Prentice-Hall, Inc., 1979).

Index

Q

Quality assurance, 117, 127
Question, 43

R

Reading, 47
Recognition, 115
Regression testing, 107, 139
Reporting
  inaccurate, 137
Retraining, 120
Rewards, 17

S

SAGE, 81
Salary, 10, 31, 33, 84, 116
Salesman, 59
Salieri, 19
Secretary, 121, 130
Seeds
  bad, 45
Service, 47, 119, 141
Site testing, 103, 107
Size
  group, 12
Smart typewriter, 126
Solutions, 43, 55, 65
Specification
  design, 77
  problem, 50, 52, 77
Stagnation, 91
Statement of work, 47
Statistician, 108
Status reporting, 137
Steering, 47
Stein, Gertrude, 43

String
  piece of, 48
Structured programming, 87
Supervisor, 11
Support jobs, 117
Support tools, 126
System test, 102

T

Teaching, 18
Tech pubs, 104
Telephone, 28
Terminals, 81
Test
  acceptance, 103
  integration, 100
  site, 103
  system, 102
  unit, 100
Test reporting, 137
Test time, 35
Test planning, 99
Testing
  document, 104
  procedure, 105
  regression, 107, 139
Tone
  management, 7
Tools
  choosing, 36
  design, 69
  support, 126
Torpedo, 47
Training subordinate managers, 21
Training, 18, 90
  management, 21
  for new employee, 93
  non-managers, 22
  for programming, 91
Transfers, 24